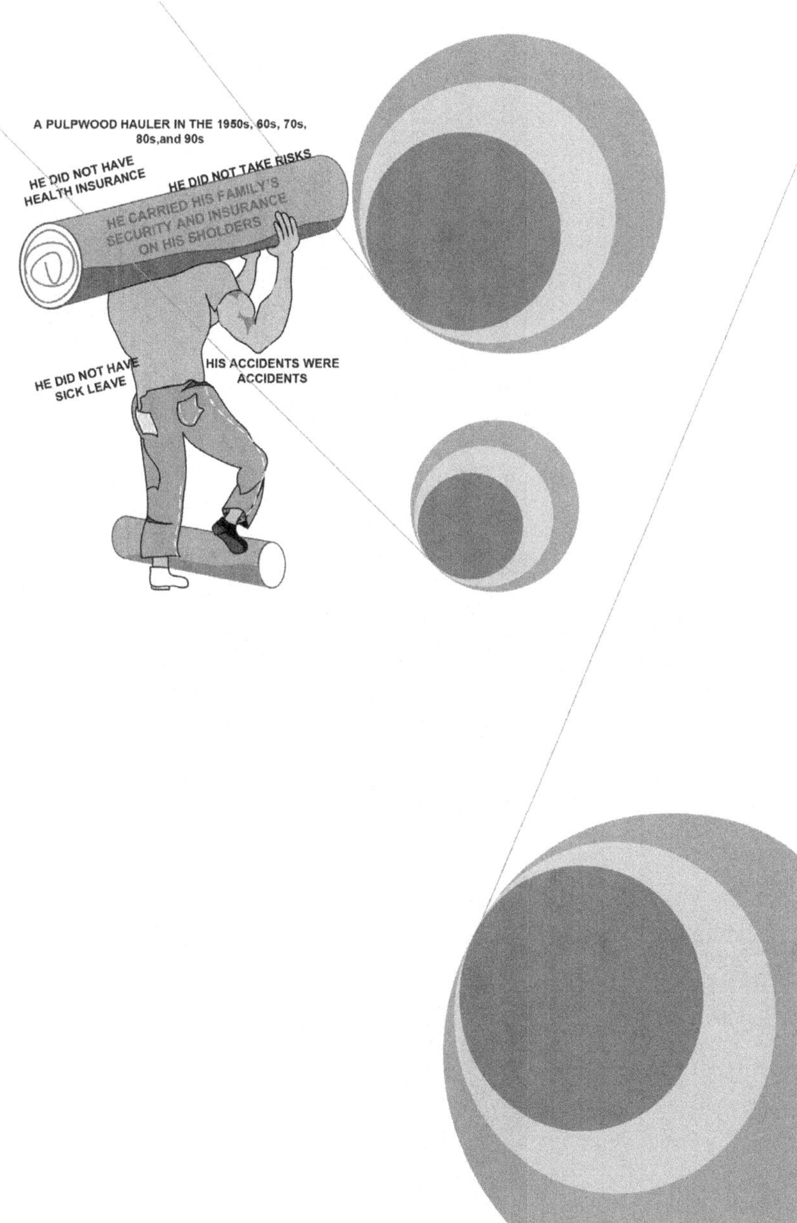
A PULPWOOD HAULER IN THE 1950s, 60s, 70s, 80s,and 90s
HE DID NOT HAVE HEALTH INSURANCE
HE DID NOT TAKE RISKS
HE CARRIED HIS FAMILY'S SECURITY AND INSURANCE ON HIS SHOLDERS
HE DID NOT HAVE SICK LEAVE
HIS ACCIDENTS WERE ACCIDENTS

Things Seen and Heard by Many

LIFE EXPERIENCES

W. THOMAS LOVE

iUniverse®

THINGS SEEN AND HEARD BY MANY
LIFE EXPERIENCES

iUniverse books may be ordered through booksellers or by contacting:

iUniverse
1663 Liberty Drive
Bloomington, IN 47403
www.iuniverse.com
1-800-Authors (1-800-288-4677)

ISBN: 978-1-4917-4465-9 (sc)
ISBN: 978-1-4917-4466-6 (hc)
ISBN: 978-1-4917-4467-3 (e)

Library of Congress Control Number: 2014949580

Print information available on the last page.

iUniverse rev. date: 04/13/2015

Dedication

This book is dedicated to two very special people who brought joy to my life: Dr. Claude McGowan and Dr. Sharifa Tahirah Love-Rutledge. Dr. Claude and my daughter Sharifa have helped me to carry many burdens. They have lifted me up when the chaos of the world has pulled me down. I know that they were sent by God with the message, "Keep the faith. You are not alone." Thank you, Dr. Claude and Dr. Sharifa! I love you with a heart that is approved and blessed by God.

Contents

Introduction

Things Seen and Heard by Many

Communication is based on experience, and many times the words leave one wondering about the history of what is said and written. In some respect, we communicate life experiences. The author attempts to capture the historical value of common expressions and reactions that we label as "life experiences," the emotion of the moment, and the outward expressions of a cotton picker. He attempted to interpret his life and feelings about his life. Life experiences change with each generation, and the author feels compelled to record them before they are lost. Often, when the moment seems joyous, a feeling of pain lies beneath the smile, a message from a soul that was seeking relief. Although problems are a way of life, we must remember this earth was cursed when the first man sinned (Genesis 3:17-19).

This book is a result of action or better yet it is a reaction to the life experiences of many people. It is the results of the author's observing people as they go through their daily life, unaware that they are being observed. The author seeks to bring to the surface the fact that within each observed life is a central problem caused by outside influences or internal conflicts. This, in turn will stimulate all who read the book to examine themselves. This examination should minimize the problems before they become uncontrollable. An uncontrolled problem will disrupt life.

There is very little optimism in this book because life primarily involves brokenness and problems. Much of art and music is based on pain and brokenness.
The world is a hard place that creates hard hearts.

Churches have many problems today and are dying of self-inflicted wounds. People have become routine and ritualistic. They have a set form of worship that can not include the personal input that is inspired by the Holy Spirit. Worshipping is time-based with man setting the criterion for God's acceptance. The Church watches sin grow exponentially and continues with a lackadaisical or an apathetic attitude. This book contains the essence of the human soul on its journey through life. We encounter many souls in our walk through this life. The book contains their joys, pains, struggles, disappointments, and sadness. Many experienced sadness and did not understand it to be abnormal. This is not a perfect world and was never meant to be after the fall of first man, but it could be much better. When we do not accept the sadness of this world, we are motivated to change. The first poem in this collection is centered on a major problem: the hypocrisy of the church.

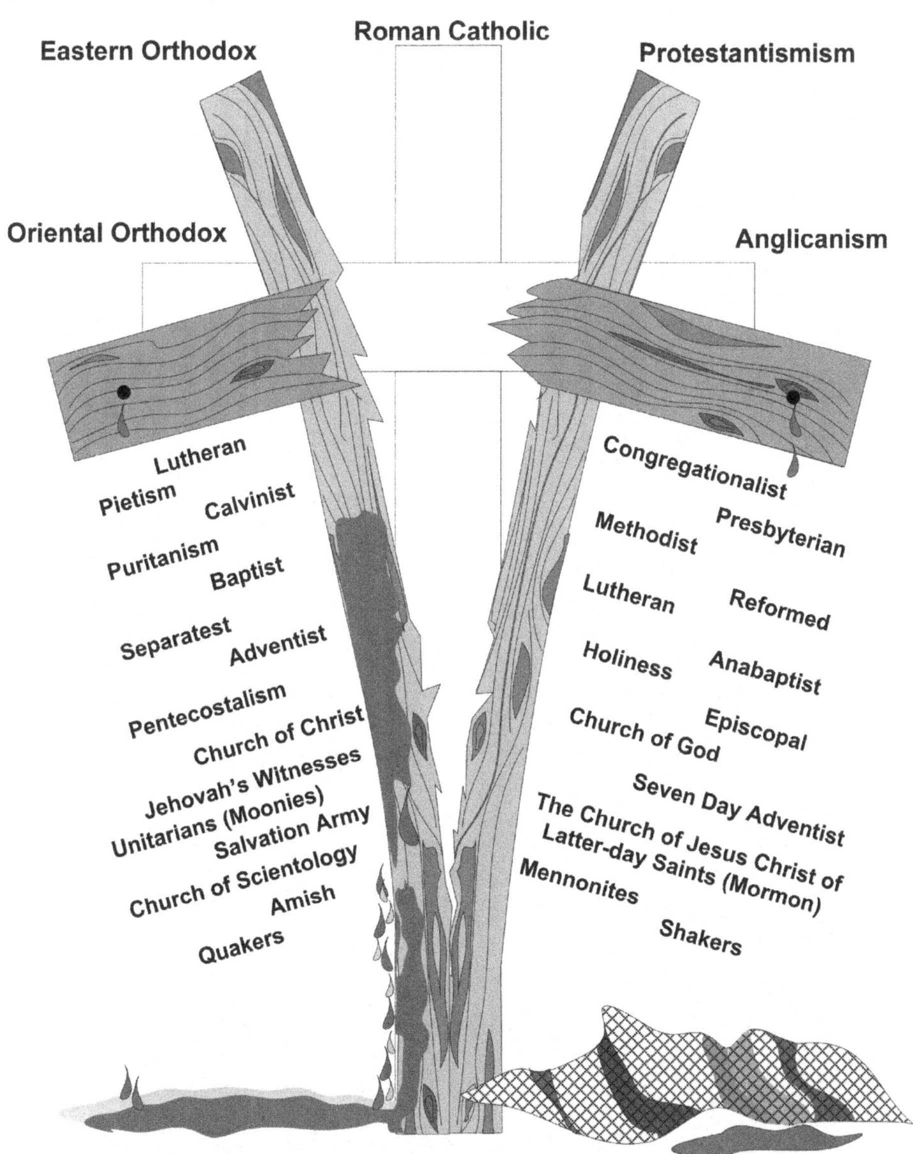

Can we fix it or do we need to?

Is the TRUTH lost among the Chaos?

Figure 1 – The Broken Cross

I The Church

I observed ninety churches from 2003 and 2008. I saw only one church's Sunday school that properly represented its membership. That church was Bartholomew M.B. Church of Garlandville, Mississippi, in Jasper County. Most churches had a shortage of participation from the men in the community. Sunday school is guided by a Sunday school book but most do not follow it. Most Sunday school teachers are not prepared to teach the lesson, and we end up with aimless discussions.

The church members' faith is based on attendance and not on sound doctrinal action. The Great Commission is never emphasized. They seem to think God just wants them to show up at the church even if they are late. It looks as though they have reduced God to a role equal to their mom and dad. If they love God, their emotion does not support their love. There is no spirit-filled obedience to love anyone or anything, not even God.

The Dim Church

If the church is the light of the world, why is the world so dark?
If the church is displaying love, why are babies born without hearts?

If it is fulfilling its commission, then why are so many souls lost?
How can a church be a church and stray so far from the cross?

What are the real reasons people attend church?
What are the real reasons people do not attend church?

What if the attendance reasons are one and the same?
One expects God to accept a half-hearted attempt and the other calls it a game.

A game is a game, and half-hearted attempts are common.
The true church is not a game, and half-hearted attempts will doom someone.

Tithes are not strictly used to help build God's kingdom.
Tithes are used by men to achieve a worldly position.

The man who pays more has got to be more in charge.
He owns a major part of the church building and all decisions are his to judge.

The pastor's directions take a back seat to the major shareholders.
The church has de-emphasized God and placed emphasis on the wishes of the controllers.

The controller only wishes to bring worldly glory to himself.
The Dim church's sheep blindly follow these goats to their death.

The Dim church is responsible for all the first world's ills.
A dead and decaying church is the work of men, not God's will.

You think the world is bad now? You "ain't seen nothing yet."
Death and destruction wait on the horizon, and they are a sure bet.

The church is blessed with many comforts, but the church is wasting valuable time.
The church is selfish and confused, but it still does not want to be left behind.

If the church is not righteous, all of your effort cannot make it right.
If imperfect knowledge is sent out into the world, the world will throw it back.

With an overabundance of beautiful buildings, the churches are not thankful but complain.
The churches seldom offer a genuine prayer, and God still bails the church out over and over again.

The church think it's bad now but they have not seen how bad it will get.
The corrupt church has not corrupted all of the third world yet.

What Christ stood for can manifest itself in any man.
The love of God and the love of man are written in the heart of others who aren't Christians.

Denominational fighting is caused by emphasis on a name and not the heart.
Man is not an exact copy of each other; differences are the will of God.

The major argument of the Dim church is based on semantics and ritual.
The church talks and practices God in everything even on Sunday religious festivals.

Sunday school is a timed event that starts at 9:30 and is completed one hour later.
One hundred sixty-seven hours with the devil and one hour with God are not going to make us better.

Some churches only stay for that one hour and then go home.
Twenty-three hours of God's day is left for the devil to prey on.

The Dim church does everything according to routine.
A church on automatic is doomed to fail the test.

The Dim church is routinely late for Sunday school and the main message.
Our society decays because of untimely and incomplete tutelage.

Man must be inspired to seek the truth, but where is inspiration?
Inspiration cannot be found in the Dim church because the Dim church has lost its foundation.

The Dim church has lost its way and does not know which direction to go.
An uninspired church cannot teach that which it does not know.

The Dim church has replaced God's perfection with its own superficial standards.
This world's gods have replaced Jehovah in the Dim church's heart.

The Dim church expects God to accept any vain attempts at worship.
Money takes priority over salvation as the primary reason for fellowship.

The Dim church wants members for the size and the money they bring.
There is no spirit in how they worship and no emotion in the songs they sing.

In the Dim church they do not understand the lyrics to the song.
In fact, a few words and the melody are all that are required to sing along.

The Dim church is not about seeking the lost souls.
Their half-hearted attempts have self-salvation goals.

The Dim church never examines its purpose or itself.
When this church should be going right, it continues to follow the misdirected left.

The farsighted hypocrites have the nerve to select a sin to criticize.
They see the sin in the distance and not the sin in their eyes.
Homosexuality is in the distance but fornication and adultery is in the pew.
Fornication and adultery damn more souls and cause more pain too.

The Dim church condones dating and pre-marital sex.
These sinful acts were with us long before the gays came out of the closet.

These sins have always been out in the open for everyone to see and participate.
Priority one is the sins that cause the greatest harm like the sexual sins and hate.

Every sin of man was responsible for Sodom and Gomorrah's fire.
Rampant homosexuality is an indicator of man's uncontrolled sinful desire.

This repulsive sin is supported by many heterosexual sins of the flesh.
The deviate heterosexual world with its perversion is now in a greater mess.

The heterosexual world thinks they are hiding the abnormal things they do.
What they don't know is that their pre-teens have got their vulgar books and videos too.

These arousal tools are creating the reaction they were designed to create.
Open your eyes, Church! To awaken the sinful flesh of a child is a major mistake.

Ill-prepared adults in these waters have written their name in hell.
A society that throws its children to the devil is terminally ill and has already failed.

It is just a matter of time before the end comes.
We have lost our children because the devil has won.

The self-righteous Dim church will not examine the path it has chosen to follow.
The Dim churches exist in a dark world and nobody knows which way to go.

The Dim church cannot orientate new converts to what is right.
The blind Dim church cannot lead ignorant blind converts to the light.

It is impossible to compute what it would take to bring the Dim church back in line.
The Dim church cannot repair what is not broke in their mind.

It is impossible to comprehend how long this decadence has been going on.
Each generation adds some novel moral deterioration and the sum is passed along.

It was the Dim church of early America that emphasized man's inalienable rights.
Matthew 25:31-46 implies that rights are not transferable for Red, Yellow, White and Black.

The Dim church gave the Red and Black man alienable rights and went to church.
They knew the god of money, but with the real God they were out of touch.

Generation after generation lived and died in hypocritical sin.
The Dim churches still love money more than men.

The Royal Law, "...love thy neighbor as thyself", has never played a part.
A half-hearted effort is all that is available from people with half a heart.

1Corinthians Chapter 13 is missing from the Bible of men filled with hate.
The Dim church must install Christ's New Commandment of John13: 34-35 before it is too late.

In the Dim church the cycles of dim awareness regenerates and proliferates itself.
Soon all good Christian churches will be sucked into this cycle of death.

This next section will cover some characteristics of a few churches visited. In most of the churches visited there was poor Sunday school attendance. A church with 75 members in attendance for the 11 o'clock service may have as little as 5 adult members in Sunday school. The next churches offered something unique that made them noteworthy.

1. **Doris Street Church of God (Moss Point, MS)**
2. **Mt. Zion (Enterprise, MS)**
3. **St. John of Jasper County**
4. **St. John of Moss Point, MS**

A Day of Appreciation at the Doris Street Church of God

A day that represents gratitude is also a day of appreciation.
Many times we are giving thanks to God through seemingly earthly expressions.

We honor God when we honor the righteous deeds of man.
The value of the moment is an acknowledgement that our brother's goodness is directed by God's hand.

We can esteem the creator by appreciating his creation.
When you set aside a holy day, you are thanking God for sending another holy son.

Expressions of appreciation can represent something or someone of value to you.
Loving tributes are often sent out, but love is perpetual; it will return too.

Even the thought of honoring someone is based on a quality assessment.
All praise shown to God's children is also a God's kingdom enhancement.

All of us present receive a blessing from the appreciation shown today.
Love for others is a homesteader, if you open the door it will stay.

Your love manifests itself in the time you have taken to show appreciation.
What you are really saying is "thank you Brother and Sister Cunningham for a job well done."

Father's Day at Mt. Zion

God has blessed many gifted fathers
of the Mt. Zion Community.
Each father was unique and
had his own specialty.

There was Mr. D. Hall who always looked majestic
while he was riding his beautiful horse.
Mr. Ollie Clark was an avid churchgoer
who always walked the right course.
Cousin Zep Hawkins, who lived alone but
never a stranger did he meet.
Mr. Andres McKendrick was one of God's men
who sat high in the deacon seat.
Uncle Cleve was a strong, honest, super worker
with a big heart.
Mr. Big Andres McKendrick, a dedicated holy man
who gave us all our Christian training.
Cousin Peter showed us how to seek and to excel.
Daddy Frank, a man with a big heart,
gave away far more than he could ever sell;
Mr. Joe Bester taught us valuable lessons in self sufficiency.
Mr. **Elijah** Anderson was a quiet dignified
man who epitomized peace.

Uncle Joe who gave much of his free time
to help us along the roadway.
Mr. Bud Martin taught us how to give
the Lord His day.

These are just a few of the fathers
who have passed this way.
Each one of us will leave
a legacy some day.

Whatever we leave, let us make sure
that it is good.
And may God bless Mt. Zion,
the little church near the edge of the woods.

St. John of Jasper County, MS

Deep into the green, brown and yellow woods I found **St. John**.
It is a place of God and a doorway to His home.

People come from far and near to this Holy place.
One thing they have in common is a friendly face.

This is Jasper County, MS, near the Clarke County line.
For one hundred and thirty- eight years this place has changed with time.

The building has changed and perhaps the people changed too.
But when it comes to praising God, most of the people know what to do.

Friendly is what they are and enthusiasm is what they live.
I've only visited St. John twice, but I found love; they freely give.

I found people who rank above average and some above excellent.
My time with **St. John** brought tears of joy and was well spent.

I met four wonderful deacons who were the epitome of God's "Mighty Men"
It is a good day when you find true brothers and friends.

They saw me off and set a date for my return.
There is still hope for this world is the lesson I learned.

Pastor Spencer was led by the Spirit because his decision came too fast to be his alone.
He gave the task to his four fine deacons that he could depend upon.

Deacons Terry Cooley, David Collins, C.B. Buxton and David Smith are men of "good degree, and great boldness in the faith."

Without a strong body that is bold in the faith, the head will fall and break.

The church is a team that must be synergized into a Holy mission. Every team must be encouraged to stay the course by praise champions.

Sisters Josephine Horne, Jennifer Walker and Brenda Durr are praise champions extraordinaire.
They encouraged and motivated the body and showed the body how to care.

There were many children at **St. John,** and I think they can change this world.
God's purity and man's Holy righteousness begin in the hearts of boys and girls.

The Pastor is the shepherd, but Jesus Christ is the Head.
With Pastor Tyrone Spencer's leadership this church has remained above the dead.

Yes!!! This was a good day at **St. John,** the little church in the wood.
I saw my Jesus that day, and it did my spirit good.

St. John, the Little Church of Moss Point, MS

A unique body of people with a common goal,
this body deals in the essence of the soul.

Everybody has a place and a talent to give.
They come together to learn and show others how to live.

Yes! These are the Good Ones.
This group makes up the body of St. John.

They can achieve because a good head directs this body.
Without a good head, everything comes up poor and shoddy.

In this group there are different branches that make up the whole.
All have unique talents and they are all special souls.

Christ is the head of St. John and the members are closely knit.
The choir is small, but it is as good as choirs get.

Rev. Gholar is the second head, and he does Christ's will.
The church is a success because he has the head-man skill.

Rev. Gholar is the minister who does his job well.
He pulls souls from the grasp of hell.

Rev. Gholar is Christ's assistant down here on Earth.
He is a working minister who puts souls first.

Whatever the occasion he always leads the way.
He is always on time, even on a workday.

He has brought together a church of very unique souls
but with two common motivations: they can sing and salvation is their goal.

I can tell you about some of his people, and what they offer the church.
I can't tell you about them all –I would have to write too much.

Sister Jones is the strong mother who keeps us in line.
She reminds us of our duties makes sure we are on time.

Sister White takes care of the money and the finances.
She purchases our materials and there is nothing left to chance.

Sister Williams is the official who directs the flow.
She's a nurse at times but always the keeper of the door.

And there is Karen, a role model for all the young people to see.
The way she conducts a devotion makes her a role model for old me.
And there is Adreain, an old young man,
a dynamic spirit with extraordinary maturity in his hand.

This group makes up the nucleus of a fine little church.
The church is growing because newer people are contributing so much.

The force behind the church is our enthusiastic minister.
He keeps the church flowing and won't let it falter.

It is from the head that we get everything we know.
This head has made a little church grow.

St. John has an abundance of voices that can sing a song,
songs that take you to the mountain top and songs that keep you warm.

Sister Gill added growth to this church.
She brought a worker's mind and a nightingale's voice we love so much.

Sister Norton came with great energy and expectation.
She reads her Bible, because she always has great explanations.

This is the power of a little church that is led by a saint.
They have much love to give and will welcome you among the ranks.

The head of this church promotes a positive attitude and love.
This is because the reverend's ministry is directed from above.

There are other men here to see.
Brother Rudolph has always been an inspiration to me.

Brother Dudly Colvin is becoming a stabilizing force.
His presence enriches all of us, and inspires the kids to stay the course.

Yes! St. John is a little church with lots of good features:
a great minister, a willing membership, and great Sunday school teachers.

A Sunday school that runs overtime has to be doing something right.
The discussion is long, time is short, but the Word has might.

The church has singers; it is full to the brim.
They sing everything from modern Gospel to old-fashioned hymns.

Some specialize in highs, some middle, and still some lows.
When Adreain brings this choir together, there is a smooth flow.

Sister Jones has the best projection and Sister Karen has the range.
Sister Gill's specialty is the hymns and Adreain can do anything.

Oh! Yeah! St. John makes music to go with the hymns.
We have three musicians named Phat, Tee, and Tim.

These musicians can sing too and that is a fact.
Sing well – especially that drummer called "Phat."

There are lots more people – I don't have time to tell you about them.
You need to come visit our Sunday school, and service and
sing a few hymns.

God bless this little church I know it is special to you.
God help it grow in the right way, and remain loyal too.

Rev. Gholar, you've got yourself a church –
A group of people who respect and love you very much.

GOD BLESS ST. JOHN!

God's Forerunners

They have one chief duty they perform each day.
Their gentle hands will assist you and show you the way.

Some think they are just the church's doorkeepers
John the Baptist was Christ's usher, these are dedicated people.

An usher is an official that you can lean on.
They will share your burden; you don't have to feel alone.

An usher is a forerunner, an escort who proceeds.
They can help you to your feet or help you to your knees.

They can help you with your prayer and fan you when you feel faint.
Relax when you are around an usher because these are some of God's
Saints.

I have seen them hold the fat lady when the Spirit came.
I have seen a 90-pound usherette restrain a 200 pound man.

When you come to worship they will find you a pew.
If your baby needs fresh air, they will take care of that too.

Sister William and Sister White are leaders of God's little Corps.
They direct young lives, assist others and still do a good job at the door.

Sister Turner is another usher who serves God too.
If you need a hand or a fan she will take care of you.

Then there is little Kim, a sweet little usherette.
Cario, Hawathi, and Bakari are dedicated and as good as they get.

Jamila and Sharifa occasionally lend a hand.
These are all God's ushers and by the door they stand.

Ushers are always ready to serve and never get in the way.
These are God's special people and needs a special day.

So let's all honor these wonderful people and show them much LOVE.
Remember them in your prayer, show appreciation and give them a big HUG.

II People

Next we will deal with the uniqueness of people. This next section is about people heard and seen. There is a separate section that deals with the exploits of pulpwood haulers.

1. B.T.W. (Booker T. Washington)
2. Mrs. Hall
3. Mr. Benny King's Prayer
4. Mr. Lott
5. Sharifa, My Child
6. The Dying Cotton Picker
7. The Man Who Was Assured of His Blessing
8. The Sharecropper
9. Our Auntie Edna
10. Our Brother, Dr. Claude

Booker T. Washington came with a prophet like message but nobody listened and the blacks are still caught up in chaos. God probably gave him that name because his initials were indicative of the essence of his message. Booker T. Washington, B.T.W. or one could identify him by his message, "Best to Wait." His message was simple in which he advised his newly freed people to wait on a plan of advancement before wasting their efforts on the unknown. Most of the ex-slaves had a skill that would keep them close to the land and B. T. W. was telling them to utilize what they

have in the place they currently reside before they start looking for greener pastures. His famous statement was "Cast down your bucket where you are". This is a biblical concept;

Pr 28:22 He that hasteth to be rich hath an evil eye, and considereth not that poverty shall come upon him.

Booker T. Washington was simply passing on a biblical message but it earned him the name "Uncle Tom".

Pr 21:5 The thoughts of the diligent tend only to plenteousness; but of every one that is hasty only to want.

History has vindicated Booker T. Washington; we are still chasing the riches of life and falling into poverty. The youth are still dreamers who dream of being sport stars, entertainers or a successful outlaw. Nobody has the patience to plan their lives; instead they gamble that they can make it with very little effort. A community needed a plan then and the community needs one now. Individual efforts are selfish efforts and this is what B.T.W. was warning them about. It is "Best to Wait" on a plan before moving ahead. We must have a plan that includes a total lifestyle change. Too much of our lives reflect the mentality of a slave with no hope.

B.T.W.

When you are knocked down it is "best to wait"
Wait because the bend comes before the break.

When the temperature increases,
take a step back.
"Best to wait," and analyze the situation
before the attack.

"Best to wait" to build the house.
The foundation is the first step.
A house without a strong foundation
will destroy itself.

Before you go out into the dark,
it is "best to wait" on the plan.
Death and failure wait in the dark
for an ill-prepared man.

It is "best to wait" until you know
precisely what you must do.
The future depends on planning and waiting
until the time is right for you.

"Cast down your bucket" and wait
till your right plan is in place.
The wise moves with patience,
and the fool moves in haste.

Don't pass up the brass
In your quest for the gold.
God's ordered steps are the only way
To achieve a worthy goal.

The ex-slave must choose the path
That leads to future success.
Without God in his plan
The ex-slave will never be at his best.

It is "Best to wait" and
Let a loving God lead the way.
The quest for selfish glory has led
A whole race of ex-slaves astray.

They moved in ignorance,
In the wrong direction and much too soon
Now that race is falling fast
In the inescapable abyss of doom.

They were told by B.T.W.
That it is "Best to Wait"
To move from the cotton field
To the capital was a fatal mistake.

They would not concentrate
On the skills to help them build.
The flamboyant ex-slave sought only
Riches and the big house on the hill.

"Best to wait" so "cast down your bucket"
In the land of your birth.
The future of the ex-slave depended
On the ex-slaves staying close to the earth.

This earth is your earth
And the land belongs to you.
That soul is God's soul
And is not to be abused.

B.T.W. if the power demands separation
To oppose the power now would be useless.
Direct your effort from opposition,
To separate economic progress.

Inequality and segregation must
Be exchanged for economic advancement.
Practical work skills is the best
Way to advance the ex-slave development.

It is "Best to wait" because
The ex-slaves are hated and despised
The lynching and "Jim Crow Law"
Was ruining too many lives.

"Best to wait" and uplift yourself
By economics and education
An impulsive life style leads
To poverty and destruction

"Best to wait" for the last train
To avoid the rush
When you rush social change
You will have to sit in back of the bus.

"Best to wait" and take the low road
Till you learn to climb.
An ill prepared person on the high road
Will always be lagging behind.

"Best to wait" and let God's plan
run its course
Always do your very best and
Always put the righteous first.

Is it right to force yourself
On another man if he rejects you?
He is certainly absent of love
But I question your love, too.

"Best to wait "and analyze why
You flee people who look like you.
If it is fear that makes you flee
Then fear has moved too.

Fear is faster; it has gone before
And caused you much harm.
Your new neighbor is fearful of you
Because you look like what you are running from.

"Best to wait" and analyze where
You are going and where you have been.
The cycle of life continues and
The sounds of the chains can be heard again.

The sound comes
Before the physical manifests itself.
Listen! Listen! These are
The chains of death.

Look down! There is
A chain down below.
This chain follows you
Everywhere you go.

Listen! Listen! For the sound, but it is
"Best to wait" before you move on.
Plan the future of your corrupted children
Before all your time is gone.

"Best to Wait" is all about
Planning for success.
Without a plan, inefficiency
Diminishes your best.

In an unplanned life, chaos and waste
Will take more than their share.
Wrong can never be righted and
Burdens are impossible to bear.

"Best to wait" analyze, and
Think things through
Without patience, the temptations
Of life directs you.

The ex-slave was driven by a need
To be like the slaver.
The slave did not take the time
To pull his plan and skill together.

Booker T. Washington advocated economic strength
Before integration and equality.
Education and economic self-reliance
Are the tools God will use to set you free.

B.T.W. was loved by whites
For advocating an inferior social position.
B.T.W. was condemned by many Blacks
For promoting segregation.

B.T.W. was really saying don't ruin
A new freedom with old blind ambition.
Crawling is the first step, then walking
Last comes running, but only in the right direction.

We, as a people, tried to run
Without going through the crawling phase.
Now we are a people of chaos
Who live in turmoil and shorten days.

If B.T.W. was here, he would
Shake his finger and say, "I told you so."
You are a dilapidated house with a poor foundation
And your death will be slow.

Look around, there is death
And unrighteousness everywhere.
Only God can save you now
Because only God cares.

When freedom came, the lies
About your inferiority came too.
You have lost the moral high ground
By obscuring the truth.

Which is it, the truth, a lie, or the
Figment of a treacherous imagination?
The truth is a prisoner of
Apathy, fear, greed and self-satisfaction.

Best to wait for a plan
To reveal the whole truth.
Without the truth,
Failure will follow you.

Booker T. Washington was not
An Uncle Tom.
He was the only man with a plan
To minimize the oppressive harm.

He was probably right when he promoted
It is "Best to Wait."
He knew first hand
The power of fear and hate.

B.T.W. has been vilified because
He advocated the best use of time.
He knew it would be a futile effort
To try to break the unbreakable line.

He said to accept the open hand
You will never be included in the clenched fist.
There is "too much water under the bridge"
To change this.

You must sublimate your effort
Toward becoming a strong digit on an open hand
Your life will be the sacrifice to
Justify the wrongs of a guilty man.

So, poor misguided finger
Just try to reach your God directed level.
Peace on Earth outside of God
Will never come. NO! NEVER!

The unbreakable line is not broken
But it did move in the right direction.
The moving line is now a snare
Used as a diversion and distraction.

It is "Best to wait" and figure out
Why you are not in the main stream.
If you look back, you will find
The once dry stubble is fertile and green.

Turn back and cultivate and
Nurture that which is in your ream of control.
You have lost five generations of digits
Mainly because of selfish goals.

The truth stands before you
And is manifested in your undeniable position.
To the Uncle Tom, Booker T. Washington
This is a vindication.

Mrs. Hall was a beloved teacher in the Clarke County School System. She was loved by the entire student body. I think students loved her because she would always listen to their problems. Even when kids did not come with a problem she showed genuine concern about them. She expected all the students to do something positive with their lives.

Mrs. Hall

She was a great lady and a mother to us all.
Everybody had great respect and love for Mrs. Hall.

She was a teacher who taught many of us.
She was that holy mother that every child trusted

They brought their problems to Mrs. Hall to seek her advice.
She had a sympathetic ear, a big heart, and was very nice.

She would pat you on the shoulder and tell you what to do.
You felt good with the talk, but she would hug you too.

She was a kind lady with a big heart, and tender touch.
She was our second mama, and we all loved her very much.

It is so sad she had to leave, but she answered God's call.
We should all strive to go to heaven so we can see Mrs. Hall.

Sleep in peace great lady, we will be alright.
You were a great teacher and your words had might.

Dear God we thank THEE for sending her this way.
I know it is your will LORD, but it is hard to let her go away.

She was a teacher about life, her instruction came from above.
She taught us kindness, brotherhood and love.

Goodbye our teacher, our mama, and our friend.
We are going to be good so we can see you again.

To My Second Mama
From: W. Thomas Love 4-5-97

The first time you hear Mr. Benny pray, you will understand that he is in a deep conversation with the Lord. In his later years, he did not walk so well; but he never failed to go to his knees in prayer. We would see him fall but just get up and continue on his way as if nothing happened. He was a man of God.

Mr. Benny King's Prayer

His prayer was reflective of the past.
The prayer asks how long hopelessness will last.

He struggled just to get to his knees
A humble man with a God to please.

His prayer was long because he covered all our needs.
His prayer covered gratitude and included pleas.

There was a fervor in his voice of a man who knew God personally.
He prayed for righteousness to be manifested in all of society.

Mr. Benny doesn't get around so good any more.
He walks with a limp because his hip and knees are sore.

His discomfort is there but his pain does not show.
If not for the limp we would not know.

Mr. Benny will fall occasionally but he seeks no sympathy.
Mr. Benny is on a mission to show us the way to the Holy City.

There aren't many "old time" Prayers like Mr. Benny left to show us how to pray.
If we will only listen and learn, his fervent style will show us the way.

"…The effectual fervent prayer of a righteous man availeth much."
James 5:16

Mr. Lott was a teacher's teacher and the consummate professional. Students saw no weakness; therefore, they had no excuse for not trying. His commitment was without flaws, and the students knew it was from the heart. There were no days when he did not display the serious instructor and the students came to learn. He taught long enough to say he taught some students' grandfathers. He was a teacher in the Enterprise School System prior to racial integration and remained in the system after the racial integration.

Mr. Lott

We wander through this jungle called life and look for an acceptable way out
We must go through life-be it short or long-but which way is an acceptable route.

We were created to follow a heaven directed plan
God gave the directions and he passed them from man to man.

A child is born helpless with a large mind to fill
To fill it with only the righteous things is God's will.

To nurture it while it is young is a special task of a mother.
To fill its mind with the God directed knowledge is the task of the teacher.

A teacher, like the parent, is with the child through the most impressionable years.
If the teacher or the parent should fail, somebody will weep bitter tears.

A child's mind is a reservoir, waiting to receive what flows.
The information received determines the way the child goes.

Today the green young minds are exposed to unrighteous dreams.
Their minds are filled with dirt, death, sex, and pleasures that are unclean.

Like tender shoots, their moldable minds are susceptible to repeat stimuli.
They learn to enjoy life but never learn right and wrong or the reason why.

In the good old days, the teacher was motivated to build good citizens.
The teacher isolated or negated the decadence of the corrupt men.

Mr. Lott was one of the last of the great old-time teachers.
His patience, professional dedication, and solicitous presence were motivating features.

He was a teacher with a rare and different approach.
He was serious about learning because he knew life was no joke.

He gave out assignments and expected completion to be done on time.
He gave us long poems which we had to learn and recite every line.

He brought culture to our little rural and unmotivated community.
He demanded that we dream of a world full of opportunity.

It seems that he saw our future long before the world accepted us.
He did not hold back the quality of training, he put education first.

Factory workers and pulp wood haulers did not really need to recite Shakespeare.
The immediate need for sentence structure and grammar was not clear.

Mr. Lott tried to give us the best education in spite of our limited opportunities.
He tried to add culture to the fundamentals and the ABC's.

He displayed tremendous dedication and consummate professionalism.
He knew we were not only listening but also looking at him.

I know we found some useful benefit from reciting "The Creation."
Some may eventually have addressed an audience of two and others the whole nation.

We can all feel proud that we got much of our start in Mr. Lott's class.
He instilled in us communication and people skills that will last.

He saw all of our potentials and encouraged some of us to sing.
He saw in us orators, preachers, teachers, and builders of things.

He saw many unmotivated young men and urged them to change.
His standards were high and he treated his students all the same.

The student had to do the work, for there was no other way.
His students were studious and attentive, they did not play.

A teacher is a public servant and must have a spirit-filled heart.
He is to teach us about life and show us the righteousness of God.

Mr. Lott did not preach to us; he gracefully taught us the duties of man.
He implied that in a hopeless situation you still take a righteous stand.

Prepare for the future even if you cannot see it.
Never give up, never say die, and never in a million years should we quit.

A wonderful lesson exposed to all by a teacher who passed it on.
It is time for all our teachers to become spirit filled before our time is gone.

Thank you, Mr. Lott!!!!

Sharifa is someone special. I believe she was specifically sent by God to keep me motivated. She is a child who made an effort to enrich her future by following the guidance of her parents. She consistently got her homework which allowed her to graduate above the top ten percent of her class. She would study her Sunday school lesson and ask question about the lesson. She would give a summary of the lesson when asked. She decided on her own to try out for the Junior Miss and did well; that takes guts. At the end of 2010 she was an instructor/student at the University of Alabama where she is working toward her Doctorate degree. The only thing I saw wrong in her growing up years was that she did not practice piano enough. She is a blessed child that brings joy to this world.

Sharifa, My Child

I look into your eyes and see
You are a part of me
But I also see in you a good spirit
That is free

There is an expression of love
That goes along with that friendly smile.
I know you like yourself because
You are a very happy child

I think you are great,
But I expect even more.
I want you to climb to the mountaintop
When you leave my door.

So prepare yourself and
Bring me joy in the process.
God is a God of perfection
So He is expecting your best.

So satisfy our God and
Do that which is right.
Then your dad will not worry
When his little one takes flight.

You are my joy, happiness and
The essence of my soul.
I can't make it if you don't
You see you are in control.

*Sharifa received her Doctorate degree on May 3, 2014.

Mr. King was a man close to the earth. He was a very friendly person who attended Wesley Chapel United Methodist Church. Mr. King loved the song "Blessed Assurance." A song tells a story about a man that calls the song his own.

The Man Who Was Assured of His Blessing

February 8, 1922 a baby was born with no knowledge of anything.
May 22, 2007 a man was transitioned with perfect knowledge of his blessings.

To bless a person is to fill that person with some benefit.
To fill the dark crevasses of our life is why the Comforter was sent.

This man knew the source of his blessing because he declared it every day.
He was so sure of his future that nothing got in his way.

God blessed him with peace and happiness and he blessed God with praise.
This man had the ultimate insurance that guaranteed him a secure place.

His blessed assurance states that "Jesus is mine".
He knew the Joy of the future and he would not be left behind.

He washed his life in the blood; therefore he knew his salvation was true.
He was a humble man that was submissive to the Creator and the creation too.

He was a man of perfect submission that was waiting on the Lord's return.
It was at the bottom of Jacob's ladder where he listened to God's Son.

This is where he heard the echoes of mercy and the whispers of love. This was the beginning of his story, his song and his praises to his God above.

His perfect submission allowed him to walk peacefully with his Savior, happy and blessed.
He would look beyond the clouds because his heart was filled with Christ's love and goodness.

Yes! This is Mr. Shellie Lee King's story and his song.
He went through this life on earth praising his Savior all day long.

When one can really sing "Blessed Assurance", he is confident "Jesus is mine."
Mr. Shellie walked with Jesus; therefore, he sang this song all the time.

He was an "Heir of salvation", because he was purchased by God.
His spirit merged with the Holy Spirit when he was washed in Jesus' blood.

Mr. Shellie's parents were Mrs. Minnie Lessie Taylor-King and Charlie King.
On April 10, 1943 he made Ms Mildred Maxine Thomas the wife of a King.

Mr. Shellie and Mrs. Mildred raised six wonderful children.
This is a family that got its strength from "Blessed Assurance".

Aunt Edna went home to be with the Lord in 2010 and the MT. Zion community has not been the same. We know it will never be the same but we enjoyed her while she was here. She was such a positive person. She did not dread hard work. One of her most impressive accomplishment was to take on the partnership responsibility of a sharecropper. This was unusual for females but

she accepted the role as one of the persons in charge. When she was in her eighties and somewhat ill, she did not stop cooking. I remember my last conversation with her, shortly before her death; she directed me to sit next to her. I often wonder if she was telling me she was leaving. She had an upbeat glow about her. Sometime she would touch my arm as she talked but I still do not know if she was telling us she is going to leave us. She did not leave me because she will always be in my heart. I loved that Lady and she loved me.

Our Aunt Edna

Daddy Frank would call her scrap because of her cotton picking ways.
Her working years were filled with short nights and hard days.

Of Mrs. Mary Etta and Mr. Charlie Ruffin's children, she was next to last of fourteen births.
This was a large sharecropping family that stayed close to the earth.

Aunt Edna was born September 30, 1925, seven days after the harvest moon.
Harvest time is the joyous time when the gold falls from the bloom.
In time she too would pull the profit from the bloom's stalk.
She learned that everything has a place because this is what she was taught.

She grew up in Yantley, Alabama, which is located between Pushmataha, Alabama, and Whynot, Mississippi.
She had farm chores but her main duty was to wash the dishes.

The family life was a sharecropper's life that included hogs, cattle, horses and a mule.
Education was important enough to walk 4 or 5 miles to Pleasant Hill School.

She learned the value of good work ethics very early in life.
Her time clock was not set by man, it started sometime before sunrise.

She gave her life to God at Mt. Nebo Baptist Church when she was 12 years old.
She moved membership to Mt. Zion to continue her heavenly goal.

The best food is found closed to the ground where the grass is seen.
Some her favorite foods are peaches, watermelon, sweet potatoes and collard greens.

These are the earth best food, grown where the grass want to grow.
Aunt Edna was taught how to control the grass with the hoe.

She used the hoe to thin the corn and chop the cotton.
Thinning and chopping is based on the premise "If two is too many, you must sacrifice one"

In the South there is the weather, a season, a reason and a tradition.
The tradition is when the cold come so does the hog killing season.

Aunt Edna participated in making of crackling, head cheese, sausage and chitterlings.
She placed value on all God's blessings and she did not waste anything.
She was taught how to boil corn to make hominy and boil clothes to remove the grime.
The young Aunt Edna accumulated a vast knowledge because she would need it in time.

This knowledge would have to come to the surface when she became a spouse.
She would need her vast knowledge and more to keep a house.

In was in Enterprise, Mississippi, where she met and married Uncle Joseph McGowan.
She said her goodbye to Yantley, and claimed Enterprise as her new town.

But she did not say goodbye to cotton and sharecropping.
She even picked the last of the cotton in a field which is called scraping.

For several years, Aunt took the leader's role in negotiating the sharecropping contract.
She was betting a year's income on fingers and a cotton sack.

She didn't leave the field until the job was completely done.
"Scrap" the nickname became a reality because it was earned.

The lady is old now, she hobbles when she walks.
Her face is distorted, and she hesitates when she talks.

Her head moves in a bashful motion as she talks to everyone.
She fears helplessness and seems to apologize for being born.

This old lady owes no one, but I feel she is not sure.
I have seen her works, and I know the pain she had to endure.

She was given the low road, but she made the best of what she had.
She bore, prepared and launched eight children, No apology needed, she didn't do so bad.

She was a special worker, a housekeeper, babysitter and field hand.
She also was a partner sharecropper; a job usually reserved for the man

Why doesn't the world around her give her the honor she has earned?
The aged should feel security and comfort because tomorrow it will be our turn.

The "Sharecropper" and "The Dying Cotton Picker" is a composition that has brought together unique observations of people that worked the fields. Many of the people who worked the field appear to have given up on a better life here on earth but seem to find pleasure in the little things of life. There was often seen a sparkle in their eyes from just a kind word that come from a mouth that seldom smiled or showed respect. They all smiled and even grinned when a child showed the expectation of a child. Children were expected to respect the elders and to "be seen and not heard." Plain and simple were their claims to fame. They saw no need to exaggerate in the way they lived their lives but they went to the extreme to tell folk tales. You look in their faces and you would see the potential for greatness which made you realize they are out of their time or out of their place. They try to hide it but you can feel their disappointment. They are too proud to cry because of their plight so somebody has to cry for them because this type of pain can only be washed away with tears. I have seen their pain and I have cried their tears but they will never know unless it is written in the book. Pride may be their undoing because it prevented them from fully working together to overcome the troubles of the world.

The "Dying Cotton Picker" is another person nearing the end of his life who is trying to utilize his transition from life to death as a catalyst for change in the life of his love ones. He is saying "Wake Up" and take my burden and make it lighter for all who follow you.

He is saying that each generation should improve on what is handed off to them. He is pleading with his children one last time to seize the time while there is time. He knows their lives and sees their future; therefore, he is telling them it is time to get serious.

The sharecropper is haunted by the fact she did not control that part of her life that was under her influence. She made some bad decisions and now she is remorseful and realizes her discomforts are primarily her own doing.
The Sharecropper is a picture of everyone who has some regret about how they lived their life. The Sharecropper now realize she was part of an unholy world where the desires of the flesh rules. An eighty two year old body does not feel like lusting after the pleasures of life. She tries to keep her eyes on God because she has doubt about her salvation after this earthly life is over.

She knew from religious training that living in the flesh was contrary to God's Spirit. Galatians 5:17 and Sunday school also taught her the works of the flesh (Galatians 5:19). The worried look on her face is there because she knows she did not please God (Roman 8:7-8). She fell prey to her flesh but she was also deceived by the world and by the devil (2Tim 3:13; Ephesians 6:11-12).

Her Christ has given her hope but she cannot shake the shame of a less than perfect life. Her silence is probably her greatest sin because confession is made to salvation: Roman 10:9-10. The other benefit to confession is that others will see and probably not make the same mistake: James 5:16. She will quietly close a life of many sinful mistakes at the grave. The other option is to tell those who follow that pleasure is momentary and joy will last forever. With spirituality comes shame and the shame seeks to hide. As a young child she started in the word of God but turned to sin. Now she does not know if she has time to be totally free from sin: John 8:31-32.

The Sharecropper

She stopped to wipe the sweat from her face.
She got a long way to go and no time to waste.

Cotton chopping is hot work
Two o'clock is the best time for a break.

It seems the sun has a score to settle
The sting of its rays is greater than a bed of nettles.

Today this lady is a July cotton chopper
Chopping is just one of many tasks of a sharecropper.

Yes! She is a sharecropper and a proud lady.
She entered the fields when she was a baby.

Now she is old and has not missed a step.
The middle of eighteen siblings, and now only she is left.

This July day the earth radiates like an oven.
Her skin is black as coal from the baking.

Fourscore-and two years old eyes have seen plenty.
The blood vessels are prominent and the white dingy.

In those eyes there is hope and the need to survive.
The joy of reading her bible is keeping her alive.

She works easy and sets the time and pace for everyone.
She sings about Jesus and about going home.

She talks about how she is the only one left
Sad because she has seen so much early death

Mother, sister and brother are all gone
Five children somewhere but she is alone.

She thinks there must be a reason for my life
Failed as a mother, and never a wife

Men, she has shared many loveless men
Weakness of flesh excuses her sin.

She would talk about her two boys and three girls
She bore them but now shares them with the world.

They seldom write, call or visit their mom
This is not God's will; this is what sin has done.

Fault lies within her because she did not share love
An old failure who did not listen to instruction from above.

Now she is paying for all those missteps
A lonely old sharecropper who cannot find death

She's being punished for crossing over God's line
To seek forgiveness she thought there was always time.

She realizes the damage caused by those who wait.
She damaged her children and now it may be too late.

She shared men, she shared food and she shared sin.
She did not share the one thing that counts in the end.

Love
"Love the Lord thy God with all the heart and with all
Thy soul, and with all thy mind, and with all thy strength…
Thou shalt love thy neighbor as thyself-Mark 12:30, 31

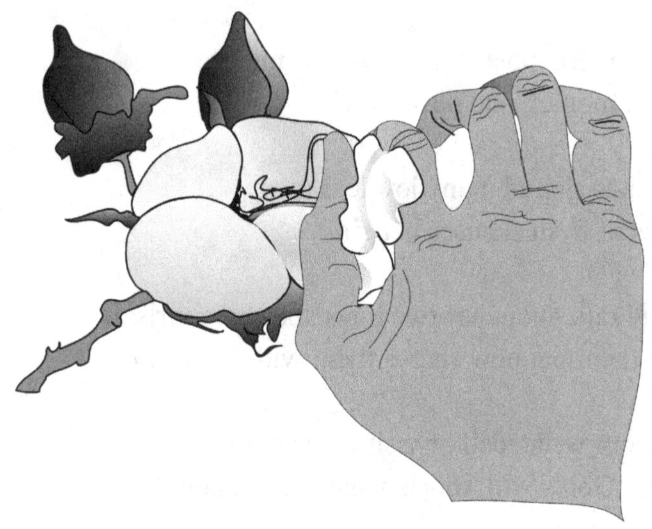

Figure 2 – Picking Cotton

The Dying Cotton Picker

The deep furrowed lines of thy face
Bring remembrance of a lonely place

That once troughed chin has lost survivability
Slowed speech is a degree of frailty

An exposing of pain from eyes that's worn
Rough callous fingers bruised and torn

This cotton picker's flame is growing dim
Death may or may not bring peace to him

Gentleness radiates from that abused face
The reality is he is ready to leave this place

The wish to leave while he's half best
God No! No cripple, not helplessness

A mountain of pride waits on death
Saying "Y'all go on, I can take care of myself"

He wants no pity, and then you feel none
This is a cotton picker, a slave's son

Death was not hard for him--no moans or groans
He peacefully closed his eyes and traveled alone

Sadness everywhere and many tears flowed
Cry not for him, he died long ago

He died of disappointment, a victim of a sin
He couldn't find righteousness in his kin

He was locked in his life and couldn't escape
But he sacrificed his life just to open the gate

He cried "Run my children! Escape! Get out of here!"
But his children continued to play, they did not care

"Escape my children! Grow and become strong."
"Hurry!" I can't hold this gate for long."

This man's heart bled until he had no blood left
Disappointment in family and people brought on this death

Disappointment is broken heartedness brought on by family
Disappointment is the injustice of a country

This cotton picker knew exploitation and misery
Pain caused by Christians who preached hypocrisy

His departure did make us all cry
But it left a void and the question, why? **WHY?**

Claude McGowan is living a borrowed life. He was not supposed to achieve the things he has done throughout his life. He is much like a Willow tree that sprouted up in the desert. There is not enough water in a desert for a Willow to grow. There were not enough of the fundamental necessities in his youthful environment to guide him to accomplish the things he accomplished. But he beat the odds and pulled himself up from a life of abject poverty to acquiring a PHD in Toxicology. The amazing thing about this is that he did this with economic hardships constantly hounding him. His life is an example of what a family can achieve if they remain supportive and remain focused on something better at the end of a testing life. He has always told himself "I am somebody" and now we all know he believed in himself.

Our Brother (Dr. Claude)

We want you to know that you, our brother, have been the highlight of our lives
You came from way down under, but you still reached for the sky.
You were born in abject poverty, an environment with defocusing means.
You were the exception to the rule because you had big dreams.
You were a quiet young man with a deep mind.

In grade school you started your self-motivated climb.
You were not distracted by the racial putdowns or uninspired peers.
You wanted something better; you were wise beyond your years.
You were guided by God; He had big plans for you.
He surrounded you with the right people and told you what to do.
Yes, we love you my brother, you have been an inspiration to us all.
You traveled a very hard road with many tormentors and pitfalls.
God gave you an understanding family that traveled with you on this road.
It takes an understanding wife and children who are willing to share the load.
Without a loving family your goal may have been unachievable.
You could have still made it but your life would have been miserable.
You have shown the young ones that they truly can excel.
You showed them dedication, you built a boat then you passed them the sail.
You showed them that they can get there from here and your life is the plan.
You made it over a hard road full of hatred and sinking sand.
Dr. Claude, we are truly proud of you.
You are our greatest Black hero and we thank God for you.
May God Bless and Keep you and your family.
May your light shine on for an eternity.

We love you Dr. Claude, we could not ask for a better brother.
No matter what happens, we will always have each other.

III Attitudes and Excuses

Dr. Martin Luther King made the statement that says a child should be judged by the content of his character rather than the color of the child's skin. I don't think anyone was really listening to what he was really saying because a child's character today says we should throw them into jail and throw away the key. The children in general today do not respect themselves. If a child does not respect himself, you cannot expect him to respect you. When Dr. King made this statement the racist world never look beyond color to locate their enemies. The racist world was not seeking friends; therefore, they had no reason to look at the content of the character of a person. This message is telling the racist to compare my wants and needs with your wants and needs and if you are a Christian, your conscience would not allow you to wish harm for others. The racist ultimate goal was to dehumanize a people by consistently putting them down. To do this the racist had to show the world everything about a subject people is bad. The racist implied they are a threat to society, they must be controlled. The only tools they knew to use are fear and terror to condition the subject people to stay in their place. This is a place of control. The system of dehumanizing a people worked because the negative effect can be seen everywhere today. A dehumanized character does not display acceptable social qualities. The racist has achieved his goal; now the subject people do not like what they have become. They must now sacrifice much of their lifestyle

to turn the dehumanizing effect off. Until then they will be judged by the content of their character and today much of it is bad. The poem "Content of Character" contains the word "Bastard." The word bastard is a biblical word, meaning it came from the Bible. It is found in Deuteronomy 23:2 and Zech.9:6. The word means all of the following:

- **Offspring of a Jewish father and heathen mother**
- **One born out of a harlot**
- **The son of a harlot**
- **Born of fornication**

The congregation of the Lord is the assembly of Israel. The bastard could mingle in the assembly but could not hold public office because of the personal defect.

Content of Character

Once a brave man stood and challenged society.
He said, "Look at me but look beyond what you perceive."

He said, "I am a man so do not kick me."
Even dumb animals feel pain when they bleed."

He said, "My heart is hurt and my mind weary."
Why does man bring so much pain and misery?

"Look at me, look – at – me! Am I what I am or
What you want me to be?
Why do you make me low?
Why are you trying to make me the beast?

You publicly judge me and you don't have the right.
I could walk on water and you will still hold me back.

This brave man said, "It is time for justice to prevail."
We have a common future whether it is in heaven or hell.

My back is weary and my soul is in a poor state of repair.
I tell you I am God's child and you say you don't care.

You have oppressed me for many, many years.
My justified anger can never be equal to your unjust fears.

My goodness is the reason why I am in this land.
There is no way you would have tolerated me as a free man.

Your lies and deceit have hurt me to the core.
Now my life is a mess, family's gone and my back's sore.

All I ever wanted to do was to let my true character live.
My untainted disposition will show you that I have much to give.

A man's character is righteous when allowed to grow like the pine.
Character is only superficially good when the character is held behind.

Your acceptance of my character may or may not be what you believe.
You now believe in your heart what started as a mean to deceive.

When can the truth be separated from the deceptions of man?
The separation starts with the exposing of the devious character-killing plan.

This brave man now focuses on his main theme.
He told the world's ears all about his magnificent dream.

The dreamer dreamed that someday his children would not be judged by color.
The dreamer dreamed that one day whites and blacks would walk as brothers.

He said judge my children by the "content of their character."
The fact about the child, not the fiction is all that matters.

What is the content? Is the content displayed, inferred or fabricated.
Character is a combination of qualities of a person that cannot be faked.

The content of one's character is good, if it is inspired by the good book.
There are distinguishing attributes that are traits of both the saint and the crook.

"You are what you are" and driven by the moral or ethical strength from within.
A body absent of the Holy Spirit has no choice but sin.

The content of man's character today is nothing to rejoice about.
Man is so evil now that even hell should kick him out.

The manifestation that distinguishes man is what he has become.
The child is reflective of the environment in which it is born.

"Even a child is known by his doings, whether his work be pure, and Whether it be right" (Proverbs 20:11.)
A child is easily led to sin, but it is very hard to bring him back.

The public estimation of a child begins with the first impression.
How he walks, his talk, and his attitude are open for interpretation.

Behind every opinion is a varying truthful fact.
The truth can temporarily be pushed aside, but it will be back.

Your character is manifested in the eyes of others by what they hear
and see.
Everybody has heard that you are dumb, shifty, lazy and carefree.

You may not care what people think, but what about the children?
When the hard task comes, then the doubt will set in.

Behind every opinion is a varying degree of truth.
An enemy takes little truth, multiplies it and gives it back to you.

If your character is bad, it is your creation alone.
God created man and gave him the means to distinguish right from
wrong.

To be judged by the content of your character has put a burden on you.
The judge may or may not use untainted facts to find the truth.

You may say you are not a thief, but can you prove it?
If you've been to jail for stealing, how does the world know you're
not guilty?

The content of your character represents what you want to be.
If there is evil in your influences, then evil is what the world sees.

There is no middle road nor is there any half-bad.
The evilness that you sing, preach and praise is very sad.

The content of your character permits a vulgar song.
Bad character creates over forty percent of the stillborn.

It is the character of a group that has filled the prisons.
The failure of so many lost souls cannot be the blame of one.

It is the group who accepts the songs and the unrighteous ways.
The propitiation of evil music and dress gives Satan praise.

Most secular music is evil, praise songs to the devil
Songs of sin that promote fornication, adultery and the will to kill.

Young men's character is to stand on the corner and blame others for no hope.
Their parents have told them the "white man" supplies the dope.

The parent says the white world wants them to fail.
They also say the United States wants them to fill all of the new jails.

The lack of good character manifests itself in no hope.
Strong healthy people stand around waiting on a daily ration of dope.

Misguided character is always influencing and training someone.
If the father's honesty is questionable, then so will be the son's.

A twelve-year-old girl has a baby out of wedlock, but there is no alarm.
We have accepted this character as the norm, so where is the harm?

Young man picks up a bicycle from right off the street.
It must have come from heaven because "my child is no thief".

Two kinds of character, one that is accepted and one that is not.
The bad character is locked away to change or rot.

Today the unacceptable live among us, and it spreads like a disease.
It is an anti-social behavior that believes in doing whatever it pleases.

This behavior will say anything, do anything and it does not matter who gets hurt.
A loveless people, hard, mean and cold to the touch.

These are devil worshippers, and they preach their gospel everywhere.
They go through town with their loud vulgar music so everyone can hear.

They wear their devil clothes so all the little children can see.
Their message is life is full of pleasure, so come little ones follow me.

Their message says that fornication is a game that even little children can play.
They also say don't worry about having babies, because we can throw them away.

Let the good times roll, sin is expected of you.
Jesus forgave the thief on the cross, he'll forgive you too.

This is the character that makes up the lost generation of man.
We taught them everything they know; now doubt rules the land.

To see a growing evil is to give approval and tolerate.
To make no effort to destroy evil is to participate.

If apathy is your solution, you are a major part of the problem.
If you truly were God's man, then your effort would be directed to solve them.

Ride on Doom Ranger you have yet to learn character kills.
Your good time comes with youth but your bad times wait beyond the hill.

Your character has everyone convinced you are bad.
I mean everyone- grandma, grandpa, your mom and your dad.

You go to the store and complain because the clerks follow you.
If it were your mom and dad's store they would follow you too.

If you look like what you say you are not, which should a wary public believe?
If you look like a thug that is all the public needs to see.

You are what you are and only you can change you.
The world is not sympathetic to the evil that men do.

Any group that has twenty five percent of its young men in jail is suspect.
Gamblers love those percentages, they are a sure bet.

For a baby to be born out of wedlock, at least two people do not care.
An unloving act multiplies, and, before you know it, bastards are everywhere.

Have you heard of a race of bastards? That is what we've become.
Facts do not lie; this is how sixty to eighty percent of our children are born.

Broken homes are not character-building environments.
The truth never hurts if you really want to repent.

You can go on living a lie and pretending there is nothing wrong.
This lie will destroy something: your or your children's home.

The character of a neighborhood is reflective of its people.
The ghetto is broken from the government to the church steeple.

Dirty buildings, dirty street, dirty officials and dirty minds.
The high road for poverty, drug abuse, bastard children and crime.

A neighborhood doesn't grow to be bad unless the people want it that way.
The ghetto is a kind of purgatory where no one plans to stay.

The black middle class sets their sight on the white suburbs.
The rest are hopeless and wait on the long black Hurst.

How can an area of a city be at fault for the things I do?
The ghetto is about the people who live there and their character too.

The ghetto can be transformed to righteousness overnight.
If all the people decided to make their character right.

You are the content of your character, not your neighborhood.
Your character adds to your community, both the bad and the good.

You are the content of your character not the color of your skin.
If you live a lie, then you give credence to the loveless men.

Stereotyping is the most dangerous part of a fiendish plan.
The content of your character is bringing joy to loveless men.

You don't know it, but you are trapped, and now Nathan Bedford Forrest smiles.
You have taken the bait and given some to your ignorant child.

To salvage your future will take a character changing effort from everyone.
You are not supposed to get out of this fire until you are done.

You are almost beyond the point of no return and don't realize it.
Your children are Godless, pleasure seekers who show no compassion or respect.
The crime rate is soaring and death comes far too soon.
The unsupervised, uncaring, unconcerned and uneducated are headed for doom.

A subtle negative change has completely desensitized you.
You can neither see nor feel the evil that is now devouring you.

The next series of poem is directed toward the attitude of the youth. "Chastity" is about the effects of premarital sex on the young girl's mind. She will never be the same because she has crossed over into something forbidden by God. The damaging effect is felt in her acknowledging she can never be clean again. She cannot clear her mind and cannot remove the body part; therefore, she is stuck with uncleanness. The value that was there is lost, so it becomes easier to share with men and to use it as a tool to achieve a purpose. The young lady has lost something that can never be regained, her innocence. The next poem goes into the effect of "Lost Innocence. The person is caught up in looking backward because she feels she has nothing up front to protect. Someone will have to bring her to reality by asking her to "Look at You."

The "cost of innocence" is based on entering an alley behind my house and accidently walking upon a male middle school teacher and one of his female students. I don't believe the young lady realize what this will cost her. They have not considered the act as unclean. It is through these unclean encounters that dreaded diseases are spread. This is not free love, there is a price to pay and both of these individual will pay. Both the male and female are sexual defile; meaning they are unclean or impure. God position on uncleanness involving copulation is found in Leviticus 15:16-18. The New

Testament calls this unclean act fornication, and fornication goes very deep in dishonoring God (1 Corinthians 6:17-20.)

Chastity

You are abused and spoiled goods
You can't stand where chastity stood.

That pedestal is reserved for those who wait
Everlasting pain comes too soon whereas, love and joy come late.

This event needs the time to let God make it right
So much misery and hurt is born In that first night.

You are abused and mentally filthy
Your mind is ravished by a society with little pity.

You would change if you could turn back time.
It is too late, promiscuity controls your mind.

You are now a slave to pleasure and sin
A thing, destined to be exploited by men.

Lost Innocence

The innocence is dead and the children are forever gone.
You must worry because they are bound for a surprisingly eternal home.

Those once carefree smiles are now filled with life's pains.
Their poison was injected into the womb by a man with no name.

These are children born for death, because of a lawless heart.
Their world is an "anything goes" world - they don't need God.

They were given life without the benefit of dad and mom.
They learn a bosom does not have to love to keep you warm.

They learn to survive with love and without regard for cost.
Their weapons make them both god and boss.

They believe that heaven is right here on this earth.
The essence of their morals is to get you first.
The innocence is gone because there aren't any mothers.
The kid can no longer tell the difference between mother and father.

There was a time when one parent wore the pants.
The X chromosome produces many males but rarely the man's stance.

Where are the childish expectations and the games we used to play?
Where is the honor and respect we practiced every day?

The future of the world depends on the children of today.
To lose the innocence of the children is throwing our future away.

Look at You

Look at you!

What are you?

Where – are - you - going?
What will you become?

What will you do tomorrow?
What is your life mission?

Why are you here?
Look at you! Look – at – you---!!

You are aged beyond your years.
You will cry many more bitter tears.

You are ignorant of your being.
Your future flashes but your mind is not seeing.

You are not a plant because you have options.

It is time to seek the right directions.

No thought is required for pleasure and fun.
The pleasure seekers are truly the lost ones.

Life was never meant to be easy, preparation removes the impediments.
Stimulating the mind and planning are the key ingredients.

Look at yourself!
What are you going to do with your life?

You have this one life of which you have total control.
Don't wait on the future, do it now! You may not grow old.

God gave you that wonderful mind to take care of you.
Take a look at yourself and do what you have to do.

God Bless!

Confused Man

When God made man, he gave him dreams that were unfulfilled.
Man always had a God to worship and land to till.

Adam was the only man born with understanding and knowledge.
As great as Adam was he still needed tutelage.

Man born of woman "is born unto trouble" and disappointment.
Most of his knowledge and understanding is not heaven sent.

Then how is man born of women supposed to survive as he grows?
God gave him mothers and fathers to tell him what he should know.

The problem with man is that he will not accept good doctrine.
Even Adam didn't listen and God taught him.

Perhaps we should question Adam's wisdom or environmental influence.
He blamed Eve but he alone failed the very first test.

We too openly play with fire and are aware of the risks we take.
Most of us are going to get burned because we've waited too late.

Adam had no role model to account for his behavior and defeat.
Most of you don't realize it but you are in too deep.

What is it? Is man stubborn or is it that he doesn't think too well?
I think man is a gambler and he is taking a chance on hell.

You see! You can tell children the way to go because you know the route.
These jitterbugs will procrastinate and completely ignore you.

One day they believe and the next day their belief is gone.
Many various opinions are leading them wrong.

Just Complaining

Don't just stand there trying to break into the locked front door, the kitchen is in the back.

Don't waste your effort trying to move where you are not wanted. Real estate has no value like the people who occupy it.

Don't just complain about the rejection and put down. Most rejection has an envious base, and that is a sin.

Don't be dissatisfied with what you are or where you've been if it was out of your control. But be darn angry at yourself if you keep making the same mistake that takes away your control.

Don't die of thirst as you look to the sky for rain. You have to go to the water, it flows down hill.

Don't continue to gripe because things have gotten so bad.
I am sure it can be turned around but change begins with you.

The weight of the world rests on your shoulders alone. Everybody stands waiting on you to make your move.

Don't dare say God is dead. Pinch yourself, you are probably dead. Dead men don't feel the pains of this earth. Dead eyes can't see the turmoil and chaos. Dead men can't love.

Don't procrastinate, right the wrong while there is still time. Wrong will never be forgotten; wrong may be forgiven but don't count on it.

"Take heed to yourselves: If thy brother trespass against thee, rebuke him; and if he repent, forgive him.
And if he trespass against thee seven times in a day, and seven times in a day turn again to thee, saying, I repent; thou shalt forgive him" (Luke 17: 3, 4.)

Do That Which Is Right!

Don't be lonely or worry about someone not loving you. Spend some time with God; He'll always be there for you. And He loves you like no mortal can.

Man is going to cause pain; he always has and always will. Crime and war is a creation of man. Man believes in all of the following and some:

- Punching somebody out
- Nuking 'em (them)
- Blowing them away
- Blowing their brains out
- Shooting them between the eyes
- Decapitating
- Hanging by the neck
- Electrocuting
- Bomb them
- Gassing
- Poisoning
- Lethal injection
- Crucifying
- Burning them alive

- Drawing and quartering

And after all that, man will kill somebody or something.

Don't worry about what people say about you. There are no perfect people.
Imperfect people will look for imperfection in you. Even imperfect people want disciples.

Don't spend your time trying to be the best in the eyes of man.
The best don't count for much anymore; it is all about relationships.

The best relationship you can form is with Jesus.
Take the time to get to know Jesus. Jesus has brought me true peace.

The Cost of Innocence

Two infernos of desire meet on a hot summer night.
Wrong is the achievement that can never be made right.

Temporary ecstasy is always a permanent mistake.
This night will determine these young souls fate.

The taint will never be cleaned and their lives will never be the same.
Many souls are responsible because ignorance is blamed.

They know and feel wrong but desire serves the means to see.
Morality is always lost in a world of apathy.

Yes! There is little care because youth have plenty of time.
But their lives are set the moment they cross the line.

After tonight innocence is lost and so is their way.
The tallyman smiles because they will have to pay.

Death and pain waits at the rendezvous. So why go outside?
The reaper's world is a dark world and there is no place to hide.

An apprehensive gift is not the givers' to give.
This trophy acquisition is against everyone's will.

Why do they do what they know is very wrong?
Sin goes very deep when it is not alone.

They have been taught there is time to forgive all faults.
Sin and seek forgiveness is what they are taught.

The sins of the mother are now the sins of the daughter.
Does God approve the path of this soon to be mother?

God's word and spirit says it is wrong but procrastinators refuse to obey.
Their forgiveness is for tomorrow, but they will pay.

Waiting on tomorrow will catch many asleep.
Death will come to all those who are in too deep.

Why does man travel such a perilous way?
Wake-up! Fornicator, you will have to pay.

Why do death and disease plagues man so?
Get real sinners! This is a debt you owe.

You can hide your transgression from me, which is easy to do.
God sees and He is going to bring hurt to you.

Birth defects, premature death, chaos and pain are what you demand.
The world's woes have been brought on by the sins of man.

A young lady crosses the line with a reluctant mind.
She is unaware of the hurt that will come in time.

A young man feels much less of a sinful wrong.
He has been taught this conquest will make him strong.

For the male, many stand and cheer him on.
But the naïve young lady will never have a trusting home.

She will be labeled as one of the easy ones.
There is no way to hide what she has done.

The spouse or boy friend will always wonder who and how many.
He doesn't count his sin and he still wants plenty.

A naïve young lady doesn't have the strength to say no.
She wants it to be the birth of love but she knows it is a score.

Not even the youth have room or privilege to make a mistake.
Just like grandma and grandpa the children will pay.

The young fools may even decide to marry.
The shadow of sin they will always carry.
Where can this mistake lead except to everlasting death?
She knows God does not approve of how she devalues herself.

Everybody places the innocent young lady on a pedestal.
The boy's devalue her environment if they can't devalue her.

In a world full of sinners is the opportunity to be unique.
But the bitter and the sour will consume everything that is sweet.

But the one thing that they must keep in mind and think about it each day,
Youthful ignorance protects them now but in time they will pay.

Some will pay today and others will pay tomorrow.
A sexually transmitted disease can work fast or slow but it always brings much sorrow.

Think about it! You got a virus in your body that's going to have its way.
No! You can't get rid of it because you have got hell to pay.

Young man thinks because of his outward appearance he is in safety zone.
You can't wash it off; it is fast and will follow you home.

I know young bodies call out for physical need.
The wrong thing at the wrong time and in the wrong way will certainly make your heart bleed.

Look around you there are sad and tormented souls everywhere.
They know there will be a lake of fire and they are headed there.

Young ones don't go through life with this tremendous burden.
Keep yourself pure, and don't give in to sin.

There are many urging you to do wrong because the righteous are few.
The miserable masses are bound for hell and will take you too.

Be a soldier for the Lord; don't sleep with the devil tonight.
God knows this world is wrong and you can help make it right.

The truth is she is only thirteen and is still somebody's baby.
Too young to give an affirmative reply or even a maybe.

Daily, these young ladies are making these life-changing decisions,
Losing their innocence and perhaps that heavenly mansion.

So these young polluted bodies will no longer be appealing.
The eyes reveal what they think they are concealing.

In time she will be too heavy and troublesome to carry.
There is no weight like the weight of a proclaimed baby.

Looseness

They call her loose, but what's loose about her?
Loose can mean not tightly fastened, not confined slack, not bound, showing a lack of restraint or responsibility, and not compact or dense in structure, and sexually unrestrained (immoral)

Each definition applies to the loose female.
All applies whether given freely or ripe to sell

Not tightly fastened, mean a dysfunctional home base
If home does not control, the desired is pulled to the evil place

Showing like of restraint or responsibility certainly applies to the loose and shoddy looseness begins with the mind and move to the body

God's law is confining and provides the restraints that binds
Everyone the law is also over the line

If you are over the line, you are also loose and out of control
One loose individual starts a chain reaction that destroys many souls.

Some think minor looseness is a quick and easy fix
Once looseness starts it may rest for a while but it never quits

It travels from person to person, and parent to offspring
Looseness is corruptible because it is a very loose thing

A loose woman has no definite shape, goal or desire
She is ready for anything because she is for hire
A loose man can never be a father because he gathers no moss
A loose life is to fluid to stay in the shadow of the cross

Good parent are tight and stays on the hill of Calvary
Fluid can't stay on a hill it flows to where Satan sleeps

Attitudes

Why do we not desire each other?
There is a negative attitude between sisters and brothers.

The attitude has probably been there forever.
The racist society forced us together.

We think we've lost this racial lever
We both should change our attitude and pull together

It seems there is no love and respect for each other.
This is one hell of a way to treat a sister or brother.

From an early age they do not want to marry and make a life.
It seems the young brother gives up very early on finding a wife

This attitude is not innate, it is learned.
There is a fear of getting burned.

All the women around him create this attitude.
Do they want a good husband or a cool dude?

There is a difference you must understand.
Your values are on the play boy, not the good man.

You placed these ideas in a growing son.
"A good man" This will not create one.

It started with any unfaithful woman.
Any woman can make an untrusting son.

It is extremely damaging if it is MOM.
The Christian woman and relatives all affect the son.
Next he experiences the promiscuous girl.
He knows this freeness is not correct for GOD's world.

These are the reasons for this attitude of the man.
The attitude comes because we deviate from GOD's plan.

The male child does not like it when the father cheats and does wrong.
If mama cheats he will never have a trusting home.

The Black man is afraid of the Black woman.
This is something every woman should understand.

One basic fear is that she is sex crazed.
This fear is instilled in him at an early age.

When dad is away from home he is earning a living.
Mom's suspicious absence is interpreted as sinning.

They know someone who is in an adulterous affair.
Sex is the number one game and fornication is everywhere.

When it comes to his woman man has a selfish heart.
She is special to him; he will not share any part.

He needs this woman who will be his and his alone.
He really wants a happy family, a good wife, and a home.

Some say, "What he doesn't know won't hurt him"
He will find hidden secrets because he is looking for them.

He will think the worst unless you prove him better.
A simple sign sometimes causes a heart to fester.

It started with a nick and it grows into a wound.
Faith is lost and separation is soon.

This is not a perfect world, man has always abused man.
He will impregnate your woman if the opportunity is at hand.

He beats his chest and feels grand.
In this war he has victimized another man.

This seems to give him some type of reprieve.
Because his eyes are saying it is going to happen to me.

He feels what his wife will do is not based on his skill.
He reads in her little faith and she has the will.

Take a look at the big picture, and you can understand them.
Man sees so many illegitimate babies that he feels the odds are against him.

It seems the game is, "make a baby and move on."
Emphasis on, "break up that happy home."

These are the reasons for the attitude of man.
The attitude comes because we deviate from GOD's plan.

What part does the woman play?
She controls the man every step of the way.

She makes him stand or she lets him fall.
She has the power because she's the mother of us all.

When we have problems we call mother.
It is she who gave us sisters and brothers.

Because of this, the young girl must understand,
What the boy child becomes is partially in her hand.

There are GOD-given responses to the male role.
The female action and reaction changes him all the way to his soul.

They each want their own special lady.
A help mate who can also give him babies.

These are GOD given instructions.
To deviate leads to destruction.

The mother has to show him the kind of woman he needs.
She instructs him and shows him with her deeds.

If she is unfaithful, even in her mind,
The boy-child believes all women are this kind.

After all who is better than the lady who gave him life?
He does not need a lady like this as his wife.

The next lady in his life is a young girl.
He is learning and she greatly impacts his world.

Remember he is looking for that special lady.
Someone to love, to honor, to obey and to give him babies.

He finds a young girl who is ignorant of her role.
Her sexuality affects all young males' souls.

She must understand the male is selfish.
There is no joy in sharing his little miss.

Questions come to mind very, very many:
Was he better than me?
Do you like him more than me?
Was he bigger than me?
How many has she been with?
Who was her first?

These questions will last a lifetime
A bad dream that slips in and out of the mind.

Whenever there is trouble or unexplained absences
It brings anxiety to all who are faithless.

The young girl must develop faith in the young man.
This can even erase the damage caused by the woman.

She must have puritan values and make him believe in her.
She must preach faithfulness in spite of her mother.

She can't be a phony, she must really believe in fidelity.
There are too many babies born out of wedlock, she can stop this tragedy.

Many believe the unwed mother is victimized
Untrue! Outside of rape she controls her life.

She decided to carry around a ball and chain.
This is because she lives outside God's plan.

Paul wrote: "It is good for a man not to touch a woman.
Nevertheless, to avoid fornication, let every man have his own wife, and
Let every woman have her own husband" (I Corinthians 7:1.)

The girl has total control in her hand
The young man will go as far as he can.

If he really likes the girl, he doesn't want her to go all the way.
This is a test to find the good girl; this is not a game he plays.

But if she gives in to this demand,
It does become a pleasure seeking game.

He did respect her and thought she was Mrs. Right.
Because of her weakness, she is his fool for the night.

A girl's virginity is her greatest asset and gives her might.
She owes this first time to her husband not some stranger in the night.

The only man to touch her body should be her husband.
It is a major sin to give in to any other man.

The virgin is "holy both in body and spirit."
She is rare and any husband she wants she can get.

The girls must understand there are no ugly girls.
Youth and virginity make hers a perfect world.

It does not matter how she looks there is beauty there.
It is her innocence that makes her so fair.

Lose her virginity then ugly sets in
The lost innocence can be seen by all men.

This is something that cannot be undone.
In her mind she feels like the dirty one.

The boy comes out smelling like a rose
He feels proud, because he just increased the rank of whores.

But the girl is in control all the way.
She must be selfish and weigh everything the boy says.

Remember the boys want to marry a virgin.
Nobody really wants a wife that's been used by other men.

This is where the attitude comes into the picture.
He thinks his wife could have been a whoredom creature.

He does not know for sure where she has been.
One thing for sure she has been with men.

The girls bring out the worst and the best.
She controls how the boys live and how they dress.

The hairstyle and the clothing is what the girls demand.
Whatever it takes to get the girl becomes part of the plan.

With this kind of power she can demand well.
The girl has the power to clean up the neighborhood.

If the girl stipulates "Do Drugs - No Me"
This would make the neighborhood drug free.

If she said "No Education - No Wife"
The dropout would get a life.

If she said "No Marriage - No Sex"
There would be no bastards and crime would be hexed.

If she would say "We must have God in our life."
The churches would be full and the communities would be nice.

The women have the power to make demands
We as a people must change - now is the time to make a stand.

The girls with a new attitude can develop the boys' attitude.
The women changing the men will not be so easy to do.

But they can see what the young people do
The change they bring will change the old too.

Ponder This

If you think fighting is ok, that is the content of your character.
Christ was not a fighter; then you will not see him in the hereafter.

Your character may tell you to pilfer or flat-out steal.
Then your character is unrighteous because of an evil will.

In class your character may cause you to be the disrupter.
That attitude comes from inside you, not from others.

Your character may lead you to say you do not care what others think or say.
God sees everything you do and, in time, you will pay.

You may pay now, tomorrow or even ten years from today.
But, as sure as there is a God in heaven, you will pay.

Teaching and learning would be easy if school was based on trust.
The content of each of your characters should produce the proper conduct.

Can anybody trust a person who refuses to do his assignment?
Imagine the character of an individual who doesn't care about advancement.

You should say I do everything I do as well as God expects of me.
You should be so proud of the content of your character, that you want everyone to see.

Your good character should display, I love everybody and myself most of all.
You should help clean up America and help right those who fall.

Your character should be so good that God will always be pleased with you.
If you will satisfy our wonderful God, you will satisfy your parents and teachers, too.

So, ask yourself, "What is the content of your character?"
God wants you to be the best that you can be, and he will reward you in the hereafter.

IV Death is Everywhere

This section will deal with some common thoughts about death, the final hour. When one believes death is eminent, it can bring tears. The tears can be tears of joy or tears of dread. Life on earth can be so vain or empty that a person will seek to leave. Life on earth can be so full of carnal pleasure the anticipating person dreads the consequences that follow death. The dread will produce pleading tears of mercy. The first poem in this death series is called "Crying Time." The death poems include the following:

- **Crying Time**
- **Doubt Beyond Death**
- **Death's Doorway**
- **Omnipresent Death**
- **Road Kill**
- **The Child Dies**
- **The Death of the Soul**
- **The Premature Departure of the soul**

"Crying Time" is about the end-times. It is a series of snapshots of the book of Revelations and what we anticipate happening when the end comes. I can see people hurrying, scurrying, and trying to make up for lost opportunity. A merciless people have enough awareness to seek mercy. The limit awareness is the beginning of

their punishment because "God shall send them strong delusions, that they should believe a lie; that they all might be damned who believed not the truth, but had pleasure in unrighteousness" (I Thessalonians 2:11-12).

The opening of the book is referring to II Corinthians 5:10, Revelation 20:12 and Romans 14:10. This poem goes through all the devastation found in Revelation.

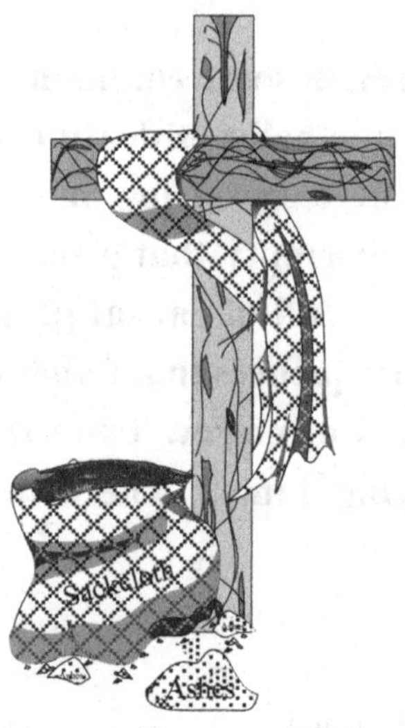

Figure 3 – Where are the Ashes and Sack Cloth?

Crying Time

More than 10,000 times 10,000 stand before the throne,
An anxious multitude seeking a permanent home.

Out there the cauldron boils and the fire burns.
Thunder and lightning will bring great harm.

The crying begins for there is the flickering shadow of the flame.
Pushing, hurrying, scurrying and now! They call out His name.

Jesus, Jesus, my Lord where are you?
Jesus, Jesus, please take me too!

Wails, moans, groans, and the wring of the hands.
The book is open with a blast and silence takes a stand.

With countenance of fear and dread, all knees weaken
Nothing else matter, salvation is what they are seeking.

In the distance is the sound of a dying earth.
Spectacular flame and monstrous lighting light up the whole universe.

As the dammed scream and run through the fire,
The multitudes call out with the voice of a mass choir.

Jesus! Jesus! My Lord where are you.
Jesus! Jesus! I want to be with you.
Jesus! Jesus! Have mercy please.
Jesus! Jesus! Please forgive me.

At the judgment they stand stacked like fish in a can,
Nobody is complaining because they now respect their fellowman.

They are all quietly listening for a name.
Fear and dread has placed fellowship in their hand.

Back on earth the call for mercy is growing very weak.
Great stress is growing and there is
Not time for rest and no place to sleep.

Hope rises like the heat and disperses like the smoke
Nobody needs a drink, and they all throw away their dope.

Half-naked women everywhere, but offer nothing appealing to men
A doomed population is too frightened to sin.

Through this chaos the trembling voices still plead
Prostitutes, pimps, murderers, and other criminals fall to their knees.

They cry! Oh yes, they cry, and cry
As loud as a doomed voice can.

Mercy Jesus, mercy Messiah, mercy God
Mercy Lord, mercy Jehovah, mercy Son of Man.
In the Ghetto the rap music is gone
The wayward father tries to seek forgiveness at home.

The gang members throw down their weapons and run for cover
The disobedient child and sinful mother seek each other.
Fear and dread is everywhere
They all realize the end is here.

The hard-hearted and cold-blooded
are calling out his name.

Jesus, my Lord Jesus I have done some good.
Jesus it is not my fault, it is the neighborhood.

Oh! Such terrible noise of a city going down
The earth shakes and men are pulled underground.

The stench of freshly torn bodies fills the air
So much blood! – And death is everywhere.

A still child's face displays no peace
Even in death its pain will never cease.

The last bigot takes no reactionary stand.
He desperately seeks his enemy's hand.

The wealthy bypass: walk, and learn to run
The fire comes because they had money to burn.

A tall man walks slowly in his priestly attire
He is in shock but he is headed for the fire.

Men struggle for a Bible to relive the pain
The masses call for mercy, over and over again.

The cry:
Forgive me, Lord! Forgive me, Lord!
Have mercy please

The crying stopped when the reality of death was at hand.
The sun became black and earthquakes shook the land.

The condemned ran to the mountain to find peace.
But from the wrath of an angry God
There is no relief.

Doubt beyond death is much like the dead rich man advising the living. This is the rich man who sought help from Lazarus the beggar in warning his kinsmen to erase the doubt about salvation (Luke 16:19-30.)

From "Doubt beyond Death" we stayed with death to identify the purpose of death which is a doorway to eternity. Every person

will go into eternity, whether it is in hell or heaven and death is the doorway.
Next, we expose the vastness of this doorway.

The poem "Omnipresent death" is saying that death could be just around the corner because it is everywhere. Then we zoom in on the death of a known friend to everybody. This friend typically expresses unconditional love. This friend is identified in "Road Kill." (John 15:13-14.)

"Isn't Anybody Going to Help?" is an accident scene n the streets of Chicago. The man lies in the street and nobody seemed to care. This accident was witnessed by a 12-year-old child. The victim was black and they took him away on a fire truck. The child was left wondering where the ambulance (1950s) was.

"A Request From Beyond" is based on the lives of Uncle Cleve Evans and Daddy Frank McGowan. They were committed workers who got the job done and were dependable. They taught me well. The biblical verses of Colossians 3:23-24 describe their motivation. They work to God's criteria.

"Time" came from many observations. Everybody is affected by time. So many things are linked to time; pain, light and dark and everything will fall when given time. The heart story is about warm feelings. It is about touching without touching. It is about saying without speaking. It is the cheer of a smile that reaches a heart. It is saying hello twenty four hours a day and seven days a week.
The heart is about family and friends. The heart is also called church or the body of Christ. This is where we find love and love always come with deep feelings.

"Family and Friends" is about close relationships typically seen in families and among friends.

Doubt Beyond Death

Play the music softly and pray the wind is still.
Shed no tears for me; I think I'm going up that hill.

You may say kind words, but let it be the truth.
Let my having lived, produce a change in you.

I did make mistakes, for I was only human.
Make amends for your mistakes, before it is out of your hand.

I am sleeping now, gone for an eternity.
If my living saves you, then my soul will know peace.

I lay here looking at the darkness, wondering if I passed the test.
Listen to me and erase the doubt. Please do your very best.

Our God is monitoring you, so don't try to deceive.
Unlike me, you can determine where you spend eternity.

So let my demise be a catalyst. Walk with your hand in God's hand.
And when death comes, your life will not have been in vain.

Furthermore, you can erase any doubt, that is, if you seek perfection.
I was satisfied with mediocrity, and now I fear the rejection

You can never be good enough because the flesh is weak.
Tomorrow must be higher than today and perfection at its peak.

So shed no tears for me, I know I did not do my best.
You need to build on my failure, and be certain you will pass the test.

Death's Doorway

Death is the doorway, the only way out of here.
The entrance is bottlenecked because of the fear.

Death is death and there is no way around this fact.
Death is final; it is the very last act.

Death may come quickly or in time.
Death, the eraser, leaves no life behind.

In death pity is self-serving and is a waste.
There is no mercy in death; it is too late.

Death can be as sudden as the lighting flash in the storm.
If you stand at the doorway, it will come.

Death is dreaded by many but welcomed by a few.
If you follow God's plan you will welcome death too.

Omnipresent Death

Death stands on the side
Of a rural road and points his finger
A car disappears beneath the brush
And a life will leave us

Death stands on the creek bank
And singles out a strong child
Water extinguishes the flame of life
And death smiles.

Death stands near a kitchen cabinet
And touches a baby's tiny arm
An eerie silence that will last forever
Is what death has done.

Death no! Death no! Don't go near
That sleeping infant's bed.
Death never looks up, he is deaf
So he touched that poor child's head.

An elderly lady called for death
To ease her constant pain.
In time he will return
But he has already taken her name.

Death walks up just in time
To witness a quarrel between husband and wife
Death pats him on the back
And passes her the kitchen knife.

Death sees two little children
Playing with a loaded gun
Death will not pass this one up because
This is an easy one.

Death takes the junkies needle
Kisses it and gives it back to him.
The junkies share their deadly needles
Because they wish to take a companions with them.

Death loves the dark,
The darkest nights are better.
Prey is not hard to find in the dark
Because at night they gather.

Death hitches a ride with a teenager
Who is in the fast lane.
Death walked through the wreckage
To make sure no life remains.

Death moves silently through
The dark side of town.
Death kissed the bottle
And passed it around.

A hopeless drunk stood and shouted,
"Death! Oh Death! I ain't afraid of you".
Death is deaf,
But he took this old skid row bum too.

In the Ghettos and barrios,
Death has set up permanent residence
The picking is easiest
Just outside of his picket fence.

Death's neighbors don't live
In the community for long.
Death's embraces, kisses, touches and visits
Inspire the neighbors to move on.

Most of death's neighbors
Have interacted with death in some way.
He's their pimp, prostitute, pusher and
Preacher that offers them pay.

Mammon is the bait
That death use to draw his neighbor in
Death watches from his front porch
As mammon entices men.

The deadly mammon kills the brain
Before giving death the soul.
A little of the deadly poison
Takes an irreversible hold.

Death brings the best
And most deadly stuff to his neighborhood.
Only the fatal attraction
Will be accepted as good.

To death, the ghetto is
The best place to live
Lots of generous people
With lots of life to give.

Generous because they have
The wrong God and hopeless life
A Godless and hopeless people
Have nothing but a soul to give.

The Ghetto is a bonanza and
Death does not stay away for long
Death comes and goes easily here
Because God is gone.

Death takes away most
Of the three score and ten years
Death leaves no void
But brings many pretentious tears.

The Ghetto is so dark
That no light penetrates even at noon.
Death has a special name
For this place, "The land of the doomed".

Death brings in drugs and alcohol
To keep his prey in a sedate state
Complacency in such a low and hopeless state
Takes away the desire to escape.

In the "Land of the doomed",
Victims prey upon victim.
Death's buddy the devil
Encourages and instructs them.

God cannot work
With a drug laden euphoric mind.
When the rapture comes,
These souls will be left behind.

Death waits; he is in no hurry.
There are doomed people everywhere.
It is getting increasingly harder
To find anybody in this world who cares.

Road Kill

I looked for him today, but could not find him anywhere.
I worry because my trusted friend is always here.

He always greets me with joy as if I had been out of town
I never had a bad day because he was always around.

He always showed concern when I would do something wrong
Even through the rain, cold and the snow he would tag along.

But I looked for him today and couldn't find him anywhere.
I worry because my trusted friend should be here.

I walked the fence row and I looked around.
I took a ride because he might have gone to town.

As I drove, extreme anxiety grew
If my friend is lost forever what am I to do?

I should have known he couldn't live forever
I took for granted he would always be there.

There beside the road, the brown contrasted the green
My sorrow grew and I wished this was a dream.

He lay still with his back to me
I prayed, God, "Don't let this be."

But I knew he was gone forever from me.
I looked into his eyes and death stared back at me.

Goodbye Friend

He's sleep now, gone before his time.
He'll be missed because he was a friend of mine.

He's on top of that mountain with nothing to dread.
I can't hold back my tears, my friend is dead.

My friend generated much warmth and it is with me today.
I will survive but this loneliness will never go away.

God bless my friend, wherever he may be.
You've blessed me, my Father, when my friend came to me.

I cried many lonely tears for my friend.
But I know if there is a heaven, we will meet again

The Child Dies

I stand and look to yonder hill
I also look at my heart
Look at me I am your will
Yes, you played the major part

I stand and look at my channel
I also look for the beginning of my rejection
You have given me far too much to handle
You did not give simple love and direction

Yes! Take a look at me; yes, look at me!
You see my failure and my death
But your ears are plugged so you can't see
You only have love and concern for yourself

Yes! I will make you cry bitter tears
Your heart will bleed as well
Your world has aged me beyond my years
You will surely spend eternity in hell

He said "Train up a child in the way he should go."
You did not have time for me
You are going to hell and you have me in tow
I have listed my misery:

Life is fragile; it will break.
You train me to terminate.

God's laws you did not stipulate.
I – have learned to fornicate.

But I learned to share my trust
Yes! Mom, I am promiscuous.

Nurturing, you let slip
And now my baby is untimely ripped.

Holiness you never showed much
You are still playing church.

LOOK AT ME! LOOK AT COLD ME!
AND THEN CLOSE THE LID

The Death of the Soul

Everyday another soul gets tired and decides to move on.
There are a thousand undisclosed reasons a soul leaves home.

Sometimes the home is physically broken and not fit for habitation.
Sometimes the home is mentally broken and is headed in the wrong direction.

Some homes arrive physically damaged beyond repair.
Even the newness of birth cannot keep a soul there.

A juvenile home is made uninhabitable by some misdeed.
Make no mistake the soul knows when it must flee.

A soul needs time to grow and to pass God's test.
A crippled soul can never achieve its very best.

The soul will hang around for a while even when it seems all hope is gone.
But when the core is rotten the soul moves from its hopeless home.

Mentally the home usually cannibalizes itself.
Physically the outside world causes the home's death.

Mentally the home puts itself in physical harm's way.
The soul is always ready to leave; it was not created to stay.

The soul can be shot out, punched out, kicked out, cut out and bled out in time.
There is no soul in a body that has no mind.

If half a mind is in the body, then the soul is only half in control.
The end will be quick, timeless and painful because death stalks aimless goals.

But when the soul is gone there is more than just another body left.
Somebody saw that animated soul long before it was frozen by death.

At a funeral it is not just another body laid out in front of the church.
There was and is a soul out there somewhere that somebody loved very much.

It is never just another body laid out under the morgue's sheet.
That is somebody's love one with the John Doe's tag on its feet.

The soul remains but mortals cannot see it, nor understand.
Death only erases the body, not the soul of a man.

What does the soul do? Where does the soul go? Nobody knows for certain.
While we moan a lifeless body, the soul stands on the other side of the curtain.

Whether the soul goes up or down, even if we knew, would it be wise to tell?
It is not for the living to discern if the soul of a body passes or fails.

One thing for certain the soul enters this world from a warm womb.
The soul moves on in search of warmth because it is cold in a tomb.

When your heart grows cold, your soul makes preparation to leave.
A warm hearted person in a very cold world allows their soul to flee.

A good soul and a good body may part company because the cold world is everywhere.
There is no peace among the cold heart but there is peace in death.

How many of the living are responsible for driving out the soul.
The world is full of life-filled bodies that are tomb like cold.

Womb to the Tomb

One day God took a cold inanimate soul and gave it the heat of life.
He set in motion an existence that He will touch at a minimum twice.

He is the beginning and the ending so all existence He controls.
A touch of His hand brought life and a beginning to a nonexistent soul.

A soul must be protected and nurtured if it is to grow to maturity.
God take care of the innocent and helpless by providing the security.

He provides warmth and comfort for the soul that begins the journey to earth.
This soul is cradled in a fetal position in a warm vessel until it is time for birth.

The first touch of God establishes a new soul in an incubator called a womb.
The last earthly touch of God will free the soul before the host go to the tomb.

From the womb we will crawl for a while.
Then we learn to walk in the footprint of a child.

We will emerge from a dark place of security.
We are allocated seventy years to grow to reach full maturity.

Between the womb and the tomb is a life time of deeds.
We do not know how we got here and we do not know when it is time to leave.

We come as a warm and cozy vessel that must be filled.
The empty vessel must be told the prime objective is God's will.

Life is never easy for a righteous soul who walks this earth.
Troubles merge with the physical body the moment of birth.

A soul must go through the valley and climb many hills.
A soul must give love until he has no more time to give.

The body emerges from the softness of flesh to be represented by the hardness of a cold stone.
Beneath the shadow of the tomb the cold replaces all that is warm.

From the womb to the tomb represents a life time of deeds.
A body can only carry a soul for a short time before it must leave.

The tomb is the end of a seemly parasitic relationship.
The bond between the body and the soul was only a temporary fellowship.

When the soul departs the body is stilled and doomed.
The soul faces the fork in the road while the body is entombed.

The direction taken is decided long before the separation of body and soul.
Deeds done in the body set the path for eternity and expose the goal.

The fork leads to a presence with the Lord or a place of silence.
The choice is reflective of the worst of a life or the best.

There is a complete loss of heat before the cold tomb.
Death is the extinguishing of a flame that was started in the womb.

There is no ardor, no zeal and no sympathy on the other side.
The tears of the living have no effect on those who has died.

The remorseful tears of the living are really shed for self.
The living is influencing the ceremony that comes with their death.

The living will seek to pay their respect for those who are bound for the tomb.
They really fear a lonely home-going if their end should come soon.

Many come to pay their respect, but it really is a down payment too.
The mourners come to morn so they can have moaners when it is due.

Remorse is only owed to a soul if it is destine for the place of silence.
There can be nothing but joy for the departed soul that has accepted God's condition of repentance.

The time from the womb to the tomb determines joy or sadness.

Deadly Rain

The greasy impression on the pane is
A sad reminder of the rain

The rain and wind brought much pain
Now the world is not the same

I can weather the wind and the pain
But the rain also brought change

The change brought the greasy impression to the pane
The hurt returns every time it rains

A face that stared out in vain
Leaves tear tracks on the pane.

A greasy face looks distorted and maimed
As perception is washed away with the rain.

Hope multiplied by hope but there will be no change
But the change came with the rain

Now not even dreams can hide my pain
Because there will always is rain

Now not even dreams can hide my pain because
There will always be rain

I know I press against this pane in pain
But blind eyes failed when death rode the rain

Isn't Anybody Going to Help

The man is down and
His life seeps through the crack.
As he slips toward the eternal
None attempts to bring him back.

His blood puddles
Like an out of control flood.
Help only watches
Because of helps' fear of blood.

"Isn't somebody going to help?"
Says a voice from the crowd.
The voice came from a distance
Because the projection was loud.

Plenty of morbid gawkers
But none would lend a hand.
Cold fearful hearts watch
As life slips quietly from a man.

Nobody checked him
Nor did they ask his name.
The real truth is
The living knows no shame.

Dumb animals change when
The hunter takes up the gun.
But even the animal shows remorse
When the hunter takes one.

The human seems to imply
“I am just glad it is not me”.
The excuse is that somehow
The man caused himself to bleed.

So what if he did or if he didn’t
Still show some sympathy.
Tomorrow is another day and
Somebody else will bleed.

What goes around will come around and
The yield is what man sows.
The good and bad of life
Is based on the debt that man owes.

A Request from Beyond

Our paths may have crossed somewhere on this earth.
You all know this occasion celebrates the opposite of birth.

Just think of the good times we may have, could have, or did share.
I would like to be remembered as a person who did care.

If you feel you owe me a smile, then pass it on.
It can't bring joy to me now because I've gone home.

You may feel you denied me shelter while I walked this land.
I am still with you in the heart of the homeless man.

You may have denied me some cool water to drink.
There is a drowning man among you, don't let him sink.

You may have refused me substance for my malnourished body.
The opportunity is there to make others healthy and hearty.

You may have passed me up as I walked home in the rain.
Let your regret be the catalyst to ease someone else's pain.

You may have cheated me out of the best years of my life.
You can pay me by helping some other soul survive.

You, with the envious heart, I know you scandalized my name.
You have sinned, confess to Jesus and remove the shame.

Edify someone else to try to compensate for your misdeed
This is the only way you can make amends to me.

You may have had your way with the forbidden spouse.
Do the right thing now by showing them to God's house.

You may have taken that which was rightfully mine.
I forgive you, but repent while you still have time.

As you make that slow march, don't look down on me.
I am with my God and you have to look up to see.

Death is a simple crossing over if you know where you are going.
Death is only dreaded if you have fear of the burning.

I kept my eyes on the prize and my faith in front of me.
Now I am in a place where I am absolutely free.
My legacy:
My life was too short I had no time to give
My task was massive, I had pyramids to build.

All my time I used wisely and efficiently.
Idle time was not given to me.

When I dug a hole I dug it deep.
You know this is my hole even while I sleep.

Before I planted a seed I would till the earth.
If the harvest is to be successful, first must come first.

On every job, God made the plan.
Satisfactory to God was excellent to man.

I did everything with love and the right way.
My righteous life on earth has doubled my pay.

V Time

This next section is all about time. We all could use a little more time because one day there will be a time when our time is gone. Titles of the time poems:

- Time
- Lost Time
- Little Time
- In just a little Time
- In the End.
- How Long for the Pain
- The Light of Time

Time

Time is but a moment measured in seconds, minutes, and hours
Time is not relative to need, nor is it influence by power.

Time is a divine gift, not meant for waste
But there is plenty of time in the holy place

Time can't be stopped and waits for no one.
Your lost time started the moment you were born.

Not much time for a tainted life but infinite time for death
You can't borrow your brother's time; he's got just enough time for himself.

If time is so precious, why waste it
We seem to think we are only losing a little bit;
a major misconception is to think we can lose a little bit

Lost Time

Time! Where has it gone?
Time doesn't creep, it rolls along.

So much you wanted to do
But time has run out on you.

A final thrust is the last move
Time takes your energy too.

You want to climb the last hill
Too late, time took your will.

Can't borrow a little time to make amends
Man is not given time to lend

My friend you have learned to procrastinate
Now your time is up
You've waited too late.

Little Time

I would love to stop and talk, but I have but "little time".
At the end of this road waits a Friend of mine.

You see there is "little time: but a lot I must do.
Frankly, you don't have time to waste- that same friend is waiting on you.

No! We don't have time to play my friend.
There is something great waiting on us at the end.

Yes! I will work my way through and perfect my life in every way.
When you have such "little time" you can't afford to lose a day.

I got some hills to climb and some valleys in front of me.
But I'm not worried about this "little time" at the end is an eternity.

I know I will have some heartache and this "little time" will bring me pain.
Because of my faith in my friend I may fall but I will get up again.

So "little to me" so "little time", why does it move so fast?
Because all tests are temporal and not designed to last

This "little time" can be a hard test but there is no problem.
Problems to the wise are easy because they have a friend to solve them.

You don't have time to waste because there is so "little time".
And I know that a friend of mine waits at the end of the line.

If you think tomorrow is promised to you, you have wasted time.
From the moment you took your first breath, you started dying.

So there is "little time "left for you to prepare to meet my friend
Even with one minute of this "little time" can mean salvation in the end.

If you're only given such a "little time", why not spend it seeking eternity.
My friend knows the way; I am following him, so you can follow me.

Let's not stop with conversion, get somebody else in this line.
Show them love and tell them they only have "a little time."

This "little time" is fleeting and always trying to shake you loose.
Just keep the faith, and my Friend at the end, He will take care of you.

Time is the essence of life, it is important to us all
Some spend two times, a time and a half time before they are called.

But all time is "little time "and must be measured well.
Time, you can't save, you can't buy, and you can't sell.

Little time can be a time of need; Grace can help a little if we believe.

The wise redeems the little time and makes every minute count.
The wise lives like Christ until their light goes out.

The wise cast no fruit before it's time to come.
The illegitimate child's' "little time" is not right the moment they are born.

The little time is rewarding if it is spent in love.
Little time" moves swiftly if it is directed from above.

Never wish for so' little time" to pass.
"Our days on earth are as a shadow" and shadows don't last.

I would love to stop and talk, but I have but "little Time".
At the end of this road waits a Friend of mine.

You see my little time may be almost gone.
Only God knows when it is time to go home.

In Just a Little Time

In just a little time
Time will stand still
Today will be tomorrow
The valley will level the hill

In just a little time
Flesh will be no more
There will be no need for rain
And the wind will no longer blow

In just a little time
Pain will move to eternity
Joy will last forever
And the Holy city will replace the sea

In just a little time
Time will stand still
Today will be tomorrow
Because it is God's will

In just a little time
Time will be no more
Death will die multiple times
And agape love will grow

In the End

There will be a reckoning in the end
The forbidder will be the forbidden in the end
The giver will be the taker in the end
The down will be the up in the end
The "out" will be the "in" in the end.
The great will be the small in the end.
The king will be the pauper.
The killer will be killed.
The unfaithful will seek faithfulness.
All this happens in the end.

The poor in spirit will be blessed.
The mournful will be comforted.
The meek will rule the earth.
The righteous will be filled.
The merciful will be rewarded.
These blessings will all be revealed
In the end

The mean will dictate the end.
A joyous time for a few but
A terrible time for many
This is the end.

How Long for the Pain

How long, how long must we cry?
How many, how many must die?

How much pain can a body stand?
Anguish and stress can kill a man.

Somebody step forward with pride.
Stop it! Too many have died.

Feel the blood; it is hot and red.
Tears flow; my brother is dead.

Cold street, hot lifeless body cooling down.
The vapors rise; this is Death's town.

A wringing heart and a loud cry
"My brother, why did you have to die?"

How long, how long must we cry?
How many, how many must die?

I am so distressed, I can't see.
I got my brother's blood all over me.

Who killed him, was it Mom or Dad?
Somebody's blame makes me so sad.

He lived by society's rules and demands.
Blame falls on every apathetic woman and man.

This life just doesn't seem fair.
I know my brother did care.

Such a brutal death for a young man.
Look at that innocent face if you can.

How long, how long must we cry?
How many, how many must die?

He was just a child with a whole life to see.
A wonderful child who would always follow me.

I cry; many tears come down.
The salt is forming on the ground.

How many young men will die this year?
Nobody is counting because nobody cares.

The Light of Time

When the light moves beneath the stone, men must be prepared to move on.

When the shadow creeps from a place unknown,
It is time's demise because time is gone.

You must realize that you are alone; accept the shadow because time is gone;
Accept the shadow because time is gone.

As the trail of light slither beneath the stone
Accept the shadow because time is gone

Bright eyes search, but the light is gone.
With no light and no time how can the soul find home.

Seekers search but how can they find the light without the light;
And their time is gone.

Futility, futility, such wasted time should have captured the light
And brought it along

Wake up grab the light before it is gone
Follow the light it will take you home

The Tall Walls Will Fall

It is walls we build, but our walls are too tall.
The walls of unrighteousness are the walls that will fall.

We build houses too big for hearts that are too small.
It is these homes where the walls will fall.

We build kingdoms for man that is beyond God's call.
It is in these kingdoms where the walls will fall.

It is walls we build, but our walls are too tall.
The walls of unrighteousness are the walls that will fall.

The rich build mountains of wealth that's guarded by walls too tall.
The corrupt mammon will make the tall walls fall.

Man builds cathedrals to the heaven far beyond Babel's wall.
At these transparent shells of glory is where the walls will fall.

The selfish build walls of flesh that is far too tall.
When the mortar is made with blood the wall is certain to fall.

We build churches for man which is against God's call.
It is a false sense of security for a man whose wall will fall.

It is walls we build, but our walls are too tall.
The walls of unrighteousness are the walls that will fall.

We build walls to watch from a distance while the innocent falls.
We cannot hide the booty behind wall that will fall.

King Solomon rested a kingdom and a house on his wall.
As he lay dying his tall wall began to fall.

Man seeks safe haven behind unrighteous tall walls.
The superficial façade with the shallow footing will certainly fall.

Men talk and preach faith and commitment but that is all.
If they don't pledge to act, their tall wall will fall.

The enduring walls are built with a pledge and a devotion to the wall.
The walls built with bricks of perseverance and mortar of commitment will not fall.

VI Feelings from the Heart

Sometimes the expressions of others include a profound statement, and you know it came from the heart. The statement seems to stay with you for a while. This next section contains works that have taken a typical profound statement and developed it. The development is the method of capturing the power of a concept in a statement. Most of these poems were developed from a simple statement or concept:

1. **A Seed Worth Planting**
2. **Commitment**
3. **Country Life**
4. **I Will Do Something Good for Me**
5. **Little Pockets of Perfection**
6. **Lost Charity**
7. **Success**
8. **The Gradualism of the Graduate**
9. **The Graduate**
10. **The Race**
11. **The Road of Life**
12. **The way Home**
13. **There is Peace in Love**
14. **You Are**
15. **A Dying Comet**

A Seed Worth Planting

We may meet great people as we travel to the other side.
The greatest are the kind ones who bring joy to our lives.

We may see so many disappointments that we think this life is a waste.
Then along comes one of God's kind angels that will brighten our dim days.

We have learned to expect the worst without waiting on the truth.
All it takes is one kind deed to show that other people care too.

Kindness is contagious and will grow if it is sowed.
Kindness is evergreen therefore it grows in hot and cold.

But! Where are those who will sow the seeds of kindness?
All it takes is just one seed and God will do the rest.

You have sowed your seed of kindness and it shall be passed along.
Many thanks to you for your kindness and may God bless you and your home.

Commitment

What is commitment?
Is it something that was heaven sent?

What does commitment mean to you?
Is it how or what you must do?

A dream needs commitment to be fulfilled.
It is commitment that guarantees the success of the will.

Commitment is a pledge to do something, be it large or small.
Every action we make should be pledged to God's call.

Then our commitment should be emotional and should be profound.
Commitment is characterized by "singleness of purpose" and a feeling of duty bound.

Commitment is a promise, a debt, a liability and yes, an obligation.
Every commitment should be to God, therefore it is devotion.

A dream is a possibility if commitment is more than a word.
It is a commitment that allows the dreamer's prayer to be heard.

Every achievement began with a dream but it is a commitment that blesses the success.
Life is full of trials and tribulations but a commitment to God's will keep us at our best.

A dream cannot be deferred if the commitment to God is true.
There still will be distracters and disappointments but God will bring the committed through.

If the dream appears to stall, then take a look at the commitments of all participants.
Question the supporting casts dedication and its perseverance.

Every endeavor must give God the reference and the glory.
Your commitment is certain to lead to failure if it is not holy.

A holy committed person evaluates to make sure he stays the course.
The unholy many times find that they are off course and in reverse.

Being obligated to be available is a liability and must be adhered to.
The committed owe the task the effort, so it is a debit that is due.

To be bound emotionally and intellectually to a course of action is what God expects of us.
We must love what we do, have faith in the possibilities and only in God trust.

We here must show that same commitment to God through our schools.
We must be about our father's business and here is where we get the tools.

Everything we do has got to be about "what is the will of God."
Our life should be his life, at home, at church, in the street and on the job.

This school is a cross road where we must take a stand.
This is where we arm ourselves to do battle with Satan.

Let this school lift you up to new heights and outfit you with the armor of faith.
You get out of it what you put into it; therefore your success is based on the road you take.

If you walk backwards in this school, then your commitment is suspect.
What you put into this school is your decision, and that it all you will get.

You can't get blood from a turnip, but God can.
To deny yourself opportunity has never been part of God's plan.

If you deny yourself the opportunity to serve God, your commitment is zero.
You are a poor student, a bad citizen and everything else about you is low.

Zero commitment is manifested is self-gratification and self-glorification.
Zero commitment means you cannot believe in the Father, Holy Spirit or the Son.

Now! Each of us knows our faults and we know what we must do.
We can build on Dr. Trotter's foundation but it is up to you.

Note: The last line of "Commitment" refers to Dr. Jessie L. Trotter who died in November 2010. He was the founder of Lift Bible College and Theological Seminary.

Country Life

Life is like the country
A place of fields, dirt roads, hills, gullies and streams

Wooden churches, old houses, hard work, and
Good and bad dreams

Like the old road, life can be dusty
Full of bumps and treacherously muddy

Like that field, Life has boundaries and
Can be productive if it is cultivated

Like that gully, it is easy to come upon misfortune
And it is hard to get out.

But life is also like the hill – with dedication and planning
You can climb and with patience and endurance and with patience...
You can enjoy the path down.

How do you negotiate a muddy road?
Be prepared. Anticipate and let Christ share the load.

Mud is slippery. It can hold you down.
Don't go through the mud, go around.

Temptation is like dust, it is omnipresent.
It falls on everyone that's on the road to heaven.

Dust gets in the eyes, so the danger appears to fade.
Dust gets sucked into the nose and leads to an early grave.

Life is like that old wooden church that seems to last forever.
The church sees men at their best.
If men could stay holy beyond the church
We would have a much better world.

All the consecrated places are durable and full of spirit.
Beyond the hold boundary is a world of putridity.

I Will Do Something Good for Me

This morning was like no other morning, with the sun came realization too.
My future lives in front of me so what am I going to do.

I can't reach back and change the past but I can control something I have yet to see.
I will seek the future on God's terms and do something good for me.

I will seek the future on God's terms and do something good for me.

I got out of bed and looked around to see what do I truly own.
Reality says, I only had time that was mine and now most of it is gone.

I finally realized that there is no material thing that belongs to me.
So, I will seek the future on God's terms and do something good for me.

I sat there on the side of my bed and asked myself, "Are you ready for today?"
Shall this day's journey be smooth sailing or will its time just drift away?

It, just now, occurred to me that all of life's decisions are very easy.
All I have to do is seek the future on God's terms and do something good for me.

As I made my way to the bathroom, my whole spirit seemed to rise.
I no longer dreaded my dead-end job, in fact, I was anxious to go outside.

I feel good about myself and I'd like to open the world's eyes to what I see.
All they have to do is seek the future on God's terms and feel good just like me.

All I have to do is seek the future on God's terms and do something good for me.

I thought as I set out to earn my pay, everything I own will be lost if today is my last day.

If you go into the future outside God's terms, it will cause much anxiety, lost time and maybe some pain.
Continuous ups and downs will complete a cycle and start all over like sunshine and rain.

Losses may include my luxury car and the big house on the hill.
Man exists on a hope and a prayer because he does not know God's will.

There is one thing I know that others cannot see.
I will seek the future on God's terms and do something good for me.

I will seek the future on God's terms and do something good for me.

I think about the spouse and just how long will we be together.
Are we on the same path to keep us together in the hereafter?

And there are the children; they will be included in the permanency of eternity.
I must show them how to seek the future on God's terms just like me.

At work, I display a new attitude that I am proud that everyone can see.
I will seek the future on God's terms and do something good for me.

At church, my spirit is high and my worship is directed from above.
I know that I receive agape love and I return an agape level of love.

The criteria for perfection escape me.
But I know I can be as good as God expects me to be.

I will seek the future on God's terms and do something good for me.

Little Pockets of Perfection

SAFE is described as free from danger.
SAFE is not a product of numbers

It is true that the safety of a person comes from others.
The others include blue and white-collar coworkers.

Being safe also means being free from risk or potential harm.
SAFE is on the road less traveled because it is the forgotten one.

SAFE is rare and it resides in a pocket called perfection.
The pockets are small and elusive but you can build one.

In this pocket are security and that warm-hearted feeling.
Access to this pocket is not through involuntariness, you must be willing.

Some identify "Safe Haven" as an area of protection.
This is only a place of "Safe Hope" not a "pocket of perfection."

The "pocket of perfection" is a place of extremes and absoluteness.
You must find or build it by raising your heartfelt effort to it best.

You must stay focused in spite of any type of distractions.
Every action must be a measured action, especially the harmless ones.

This quest is not easy and you must stay on track.
If you chase "castles in the air" you are certain to fall back.

When you renew your quest you will find your "little pocket of perfection" has changed.

Understand! It was your impetus that moved; the "pocket of perfection" remained.

If we want to be absolutely safe, we must seek a "little pocket of perfection."
Let us find these "little pockets of perfection" and call them a "safe home."

Lost Charity

My flame is growing dim
And the sand will soon be at rest
I put my trust in Him
And I withstood the test.

Ambition and desire was put on hold
Reality exposes the futility of my past.
Now He lives deep within my soul
There is no reason for time to last

I have traveled far and seen much pain.
My search for charity has taken me to the beginning.
I have been through the storm and walked through the rain
My trek is a futile journey with no ending.

So much wasted life that the ditches are filled.
The elusive charity has never been this way.
The extinguished flames are the result of the will.
Without charity the flames last for a day.

I know of charity and my flame grows dim.
But charity is more than knowledge and understanding.

Charity is the life blood left by Him.
Charity is active and very demanding.

Charity is a social entity that supports itself
But charity must have a warm heart to survive.
Charity erases the power of death.
I need your charity to keep my flame alive.

Success

Your success in life is not totally dependent
On your potential, nor your preparation

Your success is affected less by what
You can give than what you can take

Your success is not in your hand
As much as in the hand of another

Your success is based on control
You must be the controlled before
You can be the controller

Your success is centered on a perception:
Weaker than the superior and stronger
Than the subordinate
This is control!

The key to success is time and opportunity.
Attack when the time is right
And the opportunity presents itself.

A favorable impression is the benefit
Of time and opportunity

Success is guaranteed to the favorites,
So success is based on impressions.
Impression can be a true image or imitation.

Therefore success is not based on merit
But rather social anxiety and personal gain.

Putting the best foot forward works only
If someone needs a foot.
But then that someone picks the best
Of the best feet based on his comfort zone and
The foot's potential and in that order.

The Gradualism of the Graduate

God built this wonderful world in steps or stages.
God's process was an orderly process of graduated advances.

One step after another is how he laid this world down.
Each step was part of a measured series that formed the heaven and the ground.

The project was a progressive forward movement of planned completion.
To achieve the end goal each step was completed to perfection.

The steps of man must be an orderly progression within God's plans.
One forward step at the proper time is how man should advance.

Babies all over the world do not make their step until it is time.
Babies came from a dark world where everybody is helpless and blind.

The baby's first steps are made carefully and measured because the baby has no plan.
The baby's direction should come from God but delivered by man.

Gradualism is a very important part of the process.
From a world of dark blindness we each began our test.

Each graduated step is allowed a specific time to be completed.
Time runs out where the old horizon and the new horizon meet.

At each step we leave a little bit of our soul behind.
But we cannot look back because we have so little time.

From the womb we were pulled helplessly to the starting line.
Nobody told us to get up and walk, but we learned to walk in time.

Many of us stayed at the first stage far too long.
The slow starter must work harder to catch up because 'lost time' is gone.

Man can run as fast as he can but he will never catch 'lost time'.
It is the blindness and procrastination that puts man behind.

From a world of darkness a baby will soon learn to walk.
Before the baby learns to listen, he will learn to talk.

Talking before listening is the beginning of the child's trouble.
If the child is not guided toward listening, its trouble will double.

The seemly insignificant steps of a baby's graduation will be repeated many times.
An early failure can mean the child will always lag behind.

To qualify as being proficient before graduation means the child has proven success.
We monitor the baby but many unmonitored children must pass life's test.

Each level of life must be measured before the graduate can move on.
Each preceding level acts as the foundation to build upon.

Failures and setbacks follow all poor foundations.
A great house with a poor foundation is destined for destruction.

Sometimes it is best to retrace one's steps and see how one is progressing.
Stop, look and listen to identify the dangers that are coming.

If you are healthy and happy at this level, then count yourself as blessed.
There is a world full of anti-Christ's who will never pass the test.

Carefully calculate the next step because the path gets increasingly perilous.
But you will be alright if you have faith, always love, and only in God, trust.

The Graduate

We stop – Then we start
Finish one step – start of another

Death to carelessness and birth to carefulness
Mediocrity will now give way to the best

Graduation is just a step in the progression.
Your life is supposed to be a succession

You should move from this step to a higher step
To move downward is the direction of failure and death

We are not stopping we are pausing for a time
We must refocus, set new directions and clear our minds

Start tomorrow like it is a brand new day
Your survival skills are inherent so let them lead the way

You have learned much and performed well
You have been exposed to the tools that will allow you to excel

You may lack confidence because you did not perform well
You know your fault, retrace your steps and you too can excel

If you missed Val and Sal, there are other titles awaiting you
Cum laude, president, boss, mother, daddy, and mayor are just a few.

So seek your lane on this new starting line – after today the race will start
You must be ready, you don't have much time.
You have no choice you will play a part.

You can be a winner or you can be a loser.
The choice is yours to make.
Remember! You are no longer a high schooler.
You now select the steps you must take.

Every one of you is our daughters and sons.
We are looking for achievement and success.
We pray God will keep you from harm.
But you will have to be at your very best.

We say goodbye students and somewhere up there is a place for you:

- A chair with your name on it
- A job called success
- A family built on love
- A leader of great wisdom
- A God – fearing saint
- A God ordained daddy
- A God ordain mommy

The Race

I came out of the gate fast
With great ambition.

I was propelled out of the gate with
Super charged ambition. But the finish line
Kept moving with a speed equal to mines.

I shot my arrow true
The target was quick and it moved too.

The Road of Life

If you travel down that road, -- and don't know where you go, -----
You better take Jesus with you to help you carry the load.

If you don't know where you are going and don't have time to plan.
You won't have to worry if you travel with the right man.

The road is long and winding with danger ahead of you, put your trust in Jesus, He'll take you through.

If you travel down the road, and don't know where you go,
You better take Jesus with you to help you carry the load.

Careful when you cross that third hill; the devil has armed his snare.
Just stay close to Jesus; He will get you out of there.

The road is going to be bumpy, and the bridge may be torn down.
Don't give up on Jesus, He will take you around.

If you travel down that road and don't know where you go, you had better take Jesus with you to help you carry the load.

Many have gone before you and their lives are all lost. They did not seek Jesus to help them get across.

"Life" is this roadway and temptations are everywhere. Eternal Life is your destination and Jesus can take you there.

If you travel down the road and don't know where you go,
You better take Jesus with you to help you carry the load.

All along life's roadway you will pass lost souls. Keep your trust in Jesus and stay on the road.

You will see terrible sins and death will pass before your eyes. Fear not, the man who defeated death is thereby your side.

If you travel down that road and don't know where you go, you had better take Jesus with you to help you carry the load.

You may meet your brothers-Lost, disoriented, and turned around. Keep moving; you are with Jesus—don't let them slow you down.

It is hard to pass up your mother, but she tried it alone. She had the same opportunity as you, to bring Jesus along.

If you travel down that road and don't know where you go. you'd better take Jesus with you to help you carry the load.

Life is going to get hard and it will test your faith. Expect it—you will bend, but please don't break.

Your spouse and children may give up—and refuse to go on. Don't stop, you are with Jesus and He will take you home.

At the end of this road are eternal life, and the salvation of your soul. Stay with Jesus, keep your eyes on that light and you will reach your goal.

If you travel down that road and don't know where you go, you'd better take Jesus with you to help you carry the load.

Yes! Everybody is on that road but most are going the wrong way.

They need to find Jesus and the Bible will show them the way.

The Way Home

May the footprint I leave be a shining path to all those who follow
May the trail marks of my being help them avoid the sorrow

May the trail I blaze keep them in the righteous lane
May their listening ear help them avoid the pain

May the road I take lead them to an eternity
Let the way I traveled make their trek safe and the road easy

May the footprint I leave give them the assurance they will get home
May a legacy of God- fearing goodness remain when I am gone

Let my journey reveal the express way of love
Let their eyes stay focus on the light from above

May the footprint I make and the word I say rescue a child
My their innocence and gentile heart follow me the last mile

Let my tracks steer them from the rift called hell
My they be good followers and their leadership never fails

Let my path bring together the lonely and the lost
Let their so journey stay in the shadow of the cross

Let them travel with a friendly and seeking hand
Let them seek to bring along their fellowman

May my footprints lead them away from earthly temptations
May they accept the Holy Spirit complete protection

May their journey follow the road the "son of man" traveled along
This is the road I traveled; this is the only way home

There is Peace in Love

This life we lead is all about the fundamentals of love.
We can only love if we get our instruction from above.

We must first have need for love, then seek before we can find.
We must find ways to share God's love with mankind.

We must seek a lost child and a wounded man.
We must pull a drowning lost soul to God's dry land.

We must let love heal a broken body and cast away sorrow.
Where hope is weaken and depressed, we must promise tomorrow.

This life we lead is all about the fundamentals of love.
We can only love if we get our instruction from above.

We must find the broken spirit and the wounded heart.
We must join a dysfunctional family, and become a functioning part.

We must seek to glorify God and the life He gave.
We must tell a dying world that God saves.

Yes! This life we lead is all about the fundamentals of love.
We can only love if we get our instruction from above.

We must represent our God in a time of difficulty and trouble.
God has given us all a hand and we must pass it on to our wounded sister.

When trouble comes and it will, we must all take a stand.
We can never defeat hardship and trouble but our God can.

It is the love that eases the pain and wipes away the tears.
Love changes suffering to joy and build hope out of our fears.

When tribulation comes we must make the effort to reduce its effect.
We must use all the love that we got and any love we can get.

It takes our God given love to achieve healing goal.
It is God working through saints that heals the wounded soul.

Christ left a peace that will allow us to withstand the storms.
Christ's loving peace will protect you from distress and harms.

These things I have spoken unto you, that in me ye might have peace. In the world ye shall have tribulation: but be of good cheer; I have overcome the world. John 16:33

You Are---?

You are what you are; not what you want to be,
Nor what you pretend to be.
You are not what you wish to be.
You are not what you claim to be, because
you are what you are.

You will never be what you hope to be.
Hope can never be satisfied or seized.

You are what you are, but the present
will change and so will you.

Every nanosecond the living change for both the better and the worst.
You are what you are, and you can make a difference.

It is not what you are that maps your destiny.
It is what you say you are that determine your belief.

Dirt is dirt and it holds no secret value.
No matter how you hide it the truth always come through.

You can paint or cover over dirt, but it remains dirt.
If you are dirt, then you will always look dirty
because you are what you are.

Dirt can be hidden but it always comes to the surface; just give it time.
You can never be perfect but you can be as good as God expects you to be.

When God issued that soul, He called it yourself.
You have become something different, so go back to being YOURSELF.

A Dying Comet

I was a comet with a bright shinny tail
Age has finally caught up my light has begun to fail

I was a shooting star with lot of places to go
Most of my energy wasted because of a closed door

I traveled round and around trying to find a way through
I moved toward the door but the door moved too

I would slow and plan my escape
But as soon as I made my move I was always too late

In my youth I was fast and thought I could go on indefinitely
I now accept the fact time has caught up to me

I wonder how far I could have gone if I was truly free
A diverted life's destiny shall never be

VII Friends and Family

Friends and families are the core elements of a God fearing community. A society is dependent on the righteous values of friends and family to stay above chaos. We must encourage the love of friends and family to bring order to a world gone mad. The next list of poems is about friends and family:

1. **Big Brother and Little Brother**
2. **Happiness and Family Ties**
3. **My Friend**
4. **Sons**
5. **Morning Friend**
6. **Mothers**

Figure 4 - Friendship

Big Brother and Little Brother

We used to walk together in the rain.
We used to call each other bad names.

We used to make each other weep.
We used to disturb each other's sleep.

But through all you put me through,
I can proudly say I love you.

Because you are my wonderful brother,
and I wouldn't trade you for another.

You are my mother's favorite son.
Brother we will never be alone.

We will always have each other.
and I love you brother.

Happiness and Family Ties

Happiness came few and far between
Mostly troubles what I've seen.

In my life there was not much laughter.
Little joy for sibling, mother and father.

But there was some happiness that comes to mind.
Holidays and fall revival were happy times.

Happiness in early summer when school turned out.
Children running, jumping and a few did shout.

I saw happiness in daddy when my brother was born.
He was also happy about his good crop of cotton and corn.

Happiness came few and far between
Mostly trouble is what I've seen.

Mom seemed to smile when dad came home.
His return smile seemed to say sorry I stayed so long.

Mom is happy because we love to go to church.
Dad is happy too, he just doesn't smile at such.

Mom and dad were happy for our good grades.
They showed joy and pride every time we prayed.

The greatest joy came when my oldest brother graduated.
Mom and daddy tried to be emotionless, but their tears wouldn't wait.

Those tears were joy, pure 100% love and joy.
They loved all their kids, but that day they had a special boy.

Happiness came few and far between
Mostly trouble is what I've seen.

My moments of joy make me warm and happy.
Because these moments are shared with my family.

Another joyous time came our way.
It was my big sister's wedding day.

The wedding feast was festive; people came from all around.
This wedding spread joy through the little town.

In the spring we found joy in a thicket of plums.
The children shared much happiness because of summer fun.

Mom and Daddy's life was mostly work and strain.
They shared their happiness but not their pain.

They were good and deserve our dedication to right.
They work daily to take care of us and sometime all night.

Fourth of July and food but one year we worked the fields.
No food, no day off for we had weeds to kill.

Sometime the cotton field was an amusing place.
Once Daddy threw a rotten peach that splattered over my face.

He laughed till he could not see.
We all laugh as I peel that peach off of me.

Harvest time was a time of joyous anticipation.
Daddy seemed to anticipate a confrontation.

One Sunday afternoon Daddy and his old dog would sit under a big oak tree.
Daddy loved that old dog and the dog was treated like family.

The dog was frisky and happy when Daddy was around.
All the animals seemed sad when Daddy would go to town.

Thanksgiving was always a big deal.
The whole family sat for a thankful meal.

Happiness came few and far between
Mostly trouble is what I've seen.

Celebrating the minor holidays was never part of our plan
Too much work and not enough money, but we never complained.

Daddy milked the cows and worked the fields.
Mom took care of the home and cooked the meals.

We kids were not idle, we had chores to do.
We felt obligated to do our share and extra too.

Happiness came few and far between
Mostly trouble is what I've seen.

We would walk to school but we didn't mind.
We'd start a month late because of cotton picking time.

We would catch up because our parents would be pleased.
We always had GOD's help because we spend much time on our knees.

We were not rich but our comfort came from each other.
We knew we were going to make it, just to honor our father and mother.

This is the way they wanted us to live.
They gave us a home and love, that's the least we can give.

Happiness came few and far between
Mostly trouble is what I've seen.

Christmas is the last holiday of the year.
Love and happiness is everywhere.

What you have heard are the happy moments of a lifetime, there were really not many.
This family was the exception or may not exist. You have got to admit it was a good idea.
But with a little effort we could all have loving families.

Thank you

My Friend

Listen to me
Where are you going?
Where is home?
How can you be happy?
When you are all alone?

Listen to me.
Stop for a time.
Put your hand in my hand
And it will be fine.

Listen to me.
Hear me good.
I love you friend.
Everybody should.

Listen to me.
Why are you here?
Where are you going?
Stay because we care.

Why, why dread tomorrow?
It will be fine you'll see.
Trust me my friend.
Live, yes, live free.

Sons (Deon and Bakari)

A son brings strength and power to a family.
He's on a mission with direction from above.
The essence of his mission is to help those in need.
With a strong hand that touches soft love.

Yes! My son, you have a reason for being here.
God sent you to add to the goodness of his earth.
Start your work early; there is no time to spare.
My son! Whatever you become, remember you had a divine birth

Yes! You are one of God's Angels, sent to fulfill needs.
You are not to make hearts bleed.

My dad needs you to carry on his name
I need you to increase my gain.
Your family needs you to take charge when I am gone.
Your church needs you to take them to a heavenly home.

The pastor needs you to catch him when he falls.
The ill and injured expect you to heed their every call.
A little child needs you to be a role model for him.
The cripples need your strong arms to carry them.

Your mother needs your success to make her life a success.
Christians everywhere need you to help them pass the test.

My son! God made you a male child and
He expects much more of you
He made you bigger and stronger
To help you lead us through.

You must seek wisdom to help you
Complete your mission.
Life is not easy because nowhere
In the Bible is the word fun.

Replace this fun with joy and happiness
When you make your father smile
You are doing your best.

There is great expectation whenever
A boy child is born.
You are expected to be a giver whenever
Anyone needs a son.

You are expected to lead when our leader falls.
You are expected to answer all God's calls.

You are expected to be fruitful in a righteous way.
To be fruitful outside of wedlock is to fornicate.

Take this life in your hand and
Roll it into a controlled sphere.
Hold it firm, because you don't want
It to slip out of here.

Morning Friend

I see you each morning, full of life going off to work.
Yes! We speak as we pass and occasionally there is the handshake.

But are we truly Friends?

I mean God condones Goodwill
The kind of friendship you can feel.

Our greetings should express happiness
We should pass with a feeling of brotherliness.

So let's show feeling in our greeting
Brighten someone's days with Friendly understanding.

Let them know "I am there for you."
Express it in your smile and "How do you do."

"Good Morning Friend" We Love You.

Mothers

Some call them mother
Others call them mom
They are responsible for our existence.
They nurtured and kept us warm.

We shared their hearts
We took much of their time

We brought pain to their bodies.
But these loving Angels didn't mind.

They gave us our blood.
They wiped away our tears.
They cleaned our soiled clothing,
And they took away our fears.

They fed a helpless young one.
They taught us what we know.
They didn't have to do these things so well.
They did it because they loved us so.

Some call them mamma.
Others call them mom.
Just bringing us here has been a task.
Mothers have very little fun.

Their lives are made up of care, concern and anxiety.
They experience joy and pain with every child.
We need to be careful, phone home and build faith.
They have done their job, so let them rest for a while.

They are peace makers, communicators, and accommodators.
They can be teachers, ministers, and yes! punching bags.
They have a full schedule, but still have time for family.
But an unappreciative family can turn her into an old hag.

Some call her ma, others mother dear.
We call for her in time of trouble.
We know she will always be there.
She will show love and support even if trouble is doubled.

Let's honor mothers by showing some respect.
Don't do it just for today, but do it every day.
Don't hurt that mother's child
And a little of mother's love will come your way.

GOD bless all our mothers, they are special to everyone.
They keep this world moving and growing,
By supplying it with daughters and sons.

VIII Women

This next section is about the many aspects of the woman and it begins with flowers because they have beauty in common and includes the following:

1. **Flowers**
2. **Morning Glory All day Long**
3. **She Waits**
4. **The Truth about Women**
5. **Beauty and Pain**

Flowers

The Honeysuckle is a slow creeper that tends to get lost in the undergrowth.
The Rose always stands out by pushing its beauty forth.

The Periwinkle is small but it tends to come in force to get their point across.

The Daisy stands tall and void of excess so its uniqueness is never loss.

The Honeysuckle compensates for the shadow world by it beautiful fragrance.
The Rose needs no fragrance, its size and color is sufficient.

The tiny flowers always form a group of one unique color scheme.

One becomes one of many that can be easily seen.

The ground creepers have a somewhat devious plan.

The ground creepers ambush and then take a stand.

The ground creepers do not flower until it has established a foothold

The ground creepers are short and vulnerable but are bold.

The Rose looks good enough to eat; that is why it is armed.

The weapon is not a bitter taste or a foul order; it is the blood-letting thorns.

The Periwinkles' abundance of seeds makes up for its will to die.

The Mistletoe found that it is much safer if it anchors near the sky.

Phloxes and Verbenas have been plundered so much that they have lost the will to fight.
The Vanquished Morning-Glory is only active during the dark of the night.

Impatiens are fast growers because they don't have much time.

The survivalist fight back by evolving into thorn laden killer vines.

The pretty flowers use chemical weapons to limit interaction.

The pretty flowers use beauty for attraction and the thorn for rejection.

Push and pull is the flippant lifestyle of tease.

Beauty is out front, but pain is hidden among the leaves.

The flower practices discretion and does not cozy up to everything.

The beauty is for the benefactor; all other invaders receive the thorny pain.

The Marigold launches a preemptive concern when danger is in proximity.

It will fumigate the area because of danger but not for the bee.

Morning Glory All Day Long

Women are like the beautiful flower
that greets mankind every waking morning.

Before dawn, they prepare to bring sunshine
where the moon and stars have been.

They prepare a smile to share
with a renewed world.

They prepare a kind word to soothe
the troubled souls.
That sweet tender voice brings warmth
where there is cold.

Ah! They know how to smile
with a smile that calms even the Morning beast.
And they look so good that you just have to stop
to appreciate what you see.

The beautiful flowers are like a Morning Glory
that lasts all day long.
And their solicitous beauty is like
the perfect rose without the thorns.

Those wide expressive eyes say,
"Good morning, my friend."
Their alluring fragrances awaken
the spirits of half-sleep men.

Their whole demeanor says,
"I can help if you need me."
God made these special flowers
just to calm the troubled beast.

How can man have a bad day?
When there is so much pleasure everywhere?
A pleasing smile, a pleasing voice,
A pleasing sight and a hand that cares
Appreciate the Morning Glory and
you will appreciate the day.
Ignore the flower and
trouble will come your way.

To the all-day Morning Glories:
You are a special flower with a special purpose.
Your God-directed character and beauty can save us.

She Waits

She waits because her patience is her greatest claim.
She touches because God has given her a comforting hand.

She knows that in time even the tide will turn.
She waited nine months and days for her son.
She waits until everyone has had their fill.
Putting others first and waiting requires a God given skill.

And she Waits.

She sits at the school until the final bell rings.
Waiting to her has become an everyday thing.

She goes to the market and waits in line.
She waits on the red lights, traffic directors, and stop signs.

And still she patiently waits.

She waits till the washing machine fills up with water.
She waits at the piano lesson for her daughter.

She patiently waits as her children tell her about their tough life.
To soothe their troubled minds she takes them for burgers and fries.

She will wait to be served and wait till they are done.
Wait here, wait there, wait, wait, wait on everyone.

And still She Waits.

Humility, patience, and waiting should go hand in hand.
These are special qualities God only gives to a real woman.

The real woman can graciously wait and let you go first.
She patiently carries the future until it is time to birth.

God made her this way to bring happiness to the home.
When the waiting stops and patience grows thin, happiness moves on.

If she changes, then the world will change also.
If the outcome is good or bad-will depend on which way she goes.

Patiently waiting is a God given instruction primary for the woman.
Trouble comes every time she takes the role that is meant for man.

Maybe the problems we have today are all about time and love.
Nobody got time for waiting and listening to the instruction from above.

Care, concern, tenderness, sweetness, and patience are all gifts that stabilize violent men.
These qualities are delivered by a special vessel called the waiting woman.

Yes! The real woman waits and does not mind it at all.
She waits because she is answering God's call.

If she does not have time to wait now she will most certainly wait later.
She'll wait at the jail, the emergency room or as they roll out the morgue table.

There is never too much waiting for those who play the real mama role.
Waiting on the children and the husband is what saves the whole family's soul.

God made woman the assistant or the helper so she could help man follow God's plan.
If she does not wait for the direction, she has taken the role of leader woman.

She must wait.

She must make her whole family a success.
When she is watching and waiting she is at her best

The Truth about Women

God truly did make women comparable to sugar and spice.
Women represent everything lovely, sweet and nice.

He gave them the power to attract from their head to their toes.
Why he placed so much power in the physical only he knows.

Men love to look at every precious inch of them.
Man's quest to get a better view has imprisoned him.

Deceit is now interwoven in this appealing flesh.
The attraction is natural and man does not understand the test.

The trap is very simple; it is based on supply and demand.
Bountiful and beautiful are the snares that capture man.

Exposure of the over-abundant supply will increase the demand.
An addictive beauty cannot be ignored by man.

Any feminine ankle is appealing to men.
It is at the knees where lust begins.

The exposed thigh is a real or flirtatious invitation to men.
The exposer and the gawker have crossed over into sin.

The long hair of the woman is an attraction too.
The hair's beautiful purpose is also abused.

All of the woman's God-given assets are given for a reason.
To display the half-naked body and tease is not God's instruction.

To be liked is one thing, but to be desired is another.
Vulgar display is now the norm for even the wife and the mother.

It would be more fitting if men look on women as being holy.
The advertising of physical assets is looked on as being worldly.

Men don't complain not even in church.
Some men go beyond looking and move into the realm of touch.

To display one's self is say "take a look at me".
The exhibitor finds pride in letting men see.

Strange men are allowed to see what they shouldn't see.
Excitement is generated and the dream provides the release.

A woman's curvaceous outline is stimulating to men.
A little peek at the real thing will entice most to dream sin.

The power of female attraction is so strong that it moves the world.
The world's troubles started when boy met girl.

The world's main focus is heartache and pain.
The exposing of flesh is breaking just about everything.

There are broken hearts and broken homes.
There are lost fortunes and lost thrones.

There are abandoned and murdered babies.
The prostitutes look just like the holy ladies.

Would man need drugs if a pretty woman wasn't the stimulus?
She drives his inadequacies until he self-destructs.

Man wants the most desirable under his sphere of control.
The most desirable live but where – nobody knows.

She is elusive and exposes much for man to see.
She is seen for a second but then she will flee.

Poor, dumb, stupid man is forever trying to find the right one.
She shows him her cleavage, her thighs and the chase is on.

Man bypasses the covered woman just to chase a dream.
The woman who exhibits her flesh is not all what she seems.

She is nothing but the bait of a carefully laid plan.
This pretty, sweet and precious snare will trip up any man.

This game probably started when Eve's daughter arrived.
Now everyone in the whole world is helping to keep this game alive.

At one time the ankle and neck was all man could see.
Next came cleavage and then the knee.

Then more cleavage along with the thigh being exposed.
Mini-skirts and bikini tops took away ninety percent of her clothes.

Men love to look at all the beautiful parts of women.
Women are now showing all their beautiful parts to men.

I mean all their parts; nothing is left for the imagination.
The driving force for man and woman attraction is procreation.

Women have attractive curves in the front and back.
To show these curves they wear their clothes really tight.

If the pretty woman is precious, can man accept sharing her?
Even the thought of sharing the precious thing spells trouble.

Can the exhibitionist who pleases all men be satisfied with just one man?
Is an insecure marriage part of her foolish plan?

Older women expose their body to appear as young girls.
The young girl exposes her body to seek acceptance in the adult world.

Marriage has become a game that is based on looks not love.
This type of relationship is void of any instruction from above.

Even lower animals choose their mate based on how their strength is manifested.
Men and women are strange –indeed they look only for the weakness.

Yes! Women are made of honey, spice and sugar
Sweet thing attracts vermin and should always be covered.

The more man sees the more he wants to see.
Lustful desire perpetuates the game of tease.

Men can't stop looking and women can't stop exposing.
They will play this game up until the time the angel starts blowing.

Some pretty things are so proud of their body they expose their sexy curves to everyone.
She paints it up; perfume it up so she can look like a sexy mama even to her own son.

They are precious and the cost goes up as she exposes her skin.
Man will never freely share something precious with other men.

Most men will accept that which they cannot change.
They know that in time age will end this game.

Most will not expose old and wrinkled skin.
Even the cleavage is covered in the end.

Rest in peace
Your audience has gone home.

Beauty and Pain

The snare is set with a captivating lure; something beautiful that attracts the prey.
There are so many beautiful traps that will take life away.
Beauty thrives on the blind.

because the blind is easy prey.
Beauty corrupts the mind.
Beauty takes all caution away.

Many times beauty brings hurt and pain.
Cosmetic beauty is a lure that deceives.
It traps the gullible and the untrained.
Beauty destroys or brings the denied to their knees.

The made-up lady's intent is to appeal.
The aim is to redirect the focus.
This is no accident, but her will.
All must see, two people interacting is not enough.

Her good looks are meant to influence someone.
She attracts all, even the rejects.
A successful endeavor is that when the trapping is done,
what one sees is not all one gets

IX Mama

This section is the best section because it all came from the child's love for a mother. It represents years of watching a mother sacrifice her life for a child. His mother who places her child's needs above her own. The author's mother is Mrs. Bessie Grace Watkins McGowan. On Thursday, December 18, 2014, at Regency Hospital in Meridian MS, mom went to live with God. She was surrounded by her family. The list of poems tells the story of her life and includes the following:

1. **The Amazing Grace**
2. **A Mother like No Other**
3. **God Sent Me Mama**
4. **The Tree Presents the Apple**

The Amazing Grace

She was a motherless child at a very young age.
But she realized that she had a book to write, page by page.

She worked the fields and was a child who plowed the mule.
She got her training from Saint Cloud Church School.

She and her brother tended the farm while her dad worked the lumber yard.
The farm work went from sunup to sundown and it was hard.

This amazing young lady milked the cows and slopped the hogs.
She and her brother would cut the pulpwood and cut the logs.

When early March came, they would cut, pile and burn the cotton and corn stalks.
There were no school buses to get to school, so they walked.

As a child, she would get up at 4:00 am to make the biscuits.
Rising at 4:00 am became a standard for her that wasn't easy to quit.

When daylight came, they were on their way to the field.
They tried to get most of their work done before the sun came over the hill.

This amazing young lady had to leave the field at 11 o'clock to cook for the crew.
They worked in the cool of the morning and the cool of near darkness, too.

Any child who realized the need for contributing is pretty amazing.
This young lady went beyond the typical female contribution and did everything.

She assisted in cutting crossties, churned the butter and baked the tea cakes.
She and her brother picked four bales of cotton and did other hard work.

She keeps a clean house because Mrs. Laura Francis Wheaton taught her.
May 22, 1945, Mrs. Laura left to be with God because of a gall bladder.

In her leaving, she left her son and daughter in very good hands. There was the mothering of Aunt Clara and the protection of Willie Watkins.

Grace means seemingly effortless beauty or charm of movement and she is.
It also means a favor rendered by one who need not do so and she did give.

She gave the world seven children and gracefully showed them the way.
She graciously gave of her time and labor with no expectation of pay.

Yes! This amazing lady has lived a life fitting of her name.
She is a gift from God, and it is for that purpose that she came.

God's Amazing Grace shall always have the priority place in my heart.

This would be a better world if everyone had an Amazing Grace to give them their start.

A Mother like No Other

A mother like no other is God's soothing hand
A mother like no other is a help meet for man

A mother like no other leads a virtuous life
Because she is an angel and a wife

She will sit with her sick child all night long
She will gently stroke his warm brow until the fever is gone

She will change his dirty diaper and clean his runny nose
She makes sure he has a clean body and clean clothes

A mother like no other is God's soothing hand
A mother like no other is a help meet for man

A mother like no other is God's protective bosom on earth
Her priority is God's priority and she puts her children first

She riseth also while it is yet night to check her family
She'll kiss their check and stroke their brow while they sleep

Her gentle hand is guided by God as He watches approvingly from above

She is a chosen vessel that is filled with AGAPE Love

A mother like no other is God's soothing hand
A mother like no other is a help meet fit for man

A mother is never idle; her life is a divine plan
The way of the family and her children is directed by her hand

A mother like no other has a spirit like the gentle desert rain
It is the thought of her that eases the dying soldier's pain

A mother like no other determines which way a child's life goes
She will have many fulfilling moments if she teaches them to let love flow

A mother like no other can make a meal out of nothing
Children may bring her pain but to her they are her everything

She controls her children by teaching them to reject idleness
Her rewards come when her children rise up and call her blessed

A mother like no other speaks and lives the law of kindness
Her husband will certainly praise her because she has given him her best

A mother like no other will follow God's plan because it is right
She is always there in time of need because her candle goeth not out by night

She is a woman of strength and honor because she is her husband's wife
She will do him good and not evil all the days of her life

Mother, we love you, you are a blessing from our heavenly Father

You are the reason we have life, but most of all you are a mother like no other. **Happy 75th Birthday!**

God Sent Me Mama

Before I was born I was helpless and alone.
God sent me an angel to take me to her home.

When I came to this world I was still helpless but not alone.
I felt secure in the bosom my tiny head rested on.

She gently put me down to let me learn to crawl.
I was totally unafraid because mom could hear my call.

In time, she raised me to my feet and taught me how to walk.
I understood a mother's love long before I learned to talk.

My mother's love came first in this world full of fears.
It was her God directed love that protected me and minimized the tears.

I soon learned to walk but I still felt half helpless.
I also had confidence that mama would show me what is best.

At two years old, my feeling of helplessness would turn off and on.
It was at this time I learned helplessness will never be done.

As I grew I learned much about this peril filled world.
I also learned the love of a mother is a God directed love.

Then came the teen years and I learn to appreciate clean clothing and delicious meals.
Mama sent me to school and church to make sure I learned my survival skills.

Then I became a soldier boy but God and mama followed me to a war.

Every day I was away was filled with the image of mama and God standing at the door.

They told me to be careful and remember to always pray.
I am what I am because Mama's prayer and my prayer lead the way.

The war ended for me and I was sent back to this nation's shore.
Joy filled my heart when I came home because mama and God were still at the door.

They were glad to see me and the hugs lasted all day long.
It is a powerful feeling when your mama and your God welcome you home.

Mothers are special angels sent from God to show the way home.
If a child has a mother's love, they will never be alone.

A true mother's love is an Agape type of love that is sent to her from above.
She holds everything together with a glue of a steel essence called love.

The Tree Presents the Apple of Her Eyes

God made us all special long before he presented us to the world.
We were never meant to be simply classified as boy or girl.

God polished each of our souls before He sent it down from above the sky.
We were made fit to become the apple of our Mom's, Grand-mom's and Great-Grand-mom's eye.

We are fruit that is destined to regenerate ourselves.
Our mother is a tree that knows joy like nobody else.

But! She is more than a tree that provides a channel.
Each mother and child relationship is special because she is a chosen vessel.

Mothers are instructed to "take the best fruits in the land in your vessels, and carry down the man a present". Gen. 43:11
Fruits that are diverse as "a little balm, and a little honey, spices, and myrrh, nuts, and almonds are sent".

Your glorification of your God will glorify the tree from which you come.
Every fruit is given a special gift but some never develop and some wait too long.

We come together graciously and appreciatively as fruit that is three generations deep.
It is the will of God the way we always show love and gratitude to the tree.

It is the tree that has brought us through a desert land and made us the apple of her eye.
It is the tree that has nurtured us, showed us love and taught us how to fly.

The tree points the way and says, "That my fruit is good earth, take root and grow."
The tree says, "Always love my children and teach them the way to go".

Now we all gather here to tell her we have taken root because we listened well.
Only God knows our final contribution to His world but time will tell.

Each generation's mistakes will never be repeated if we confess our faults.
Mistakes and disappointment will come when we ignore what the tree has taught.

We set aside this day to honor the tree from whence we came.
She gave us a good heart and a good name.

Her greatest gift to us cannot be seen or understood by mortal man.
This gift was revealed the day she put our hands into God's hand.

X Ills of Society

This section zooms in on some of the problems of society:

1. **An Empty Life**
2. **Black Is Wrong**
3. **Emptiness**
4. **European's Rules**

An Empty Life

To live this life and give nothing is a tragedy.
An empty life leads to an empty death full of misery.

Life is much like a fertile field
Yet some life produces no yield.

A full body that lives as a hollow shell
Is always buying and producing nothing to sell.

All living things received that same royal command
The only species with the choice is man.

Pleasure has replaced the fruit of the womb
But parasites and diseases will kill the field soon.

Tainted crops from a contaminated field
Healthy sprouts are ripped out and killed.

A senseless life with senseless goals
Chooses death over an eternal soul.

In a deep sleep, unaware of the faults
Death comes and, another procrastinator is caught.

An empty soul has ended its ride
Fell short - didn't make it to the other side.

Lost in space and time called infinity land
A place of torment reserved just for man.

Black Is Wrong

So many years we have been denied
We have not noticed how the time flies.

We are caught in a cycle and don't know how we got on.
We are so hungry we don't realize Black can be wrong.

We accept the pusher because of the money.
Poor excuse for father is called daddy and honey.

There is nothing right about these men.
These suckers are responsible for the mess we are in.

We accept that Black comic on TV because he is very funny.
What's so funny when a Black man calls you nigger and monkey?

There is nothing funny about this man.
There were Blacks who sold you to this land.

We accept the prostitute because she says this is all she can do.
Being there is influencing your child to sell her body too.

This is evil and the Bible tells us this.
You are selecting from the Bible what you can live with.

The Bible is not a buffet where you select your transgressions.
They are all-wrong and prevents salvation.

Sex is good so we accept this sin.
Sex is going to send you to hell when Christ comes again.

We know unmarried sex is wrong but we give in to temptation.
Sex is approved for the young to increase the selection.

The little misses goes half-naked and shakes it down.
She shakes an aborted fetus to the ground.

The little Mr. wants to be a pimp or a pusher.
He rapes the mama and sells his sister.

The eight-year-old speaks "big boys talk"
Craves one hundred-dollar quite shoes so he can stalk.

People slapping hands and calling each other brother.
Same hands – one pair shoots – the other is murdered.

Creating life with no intention of providing.
Hungry baby cries and daddy goes into hiding.

Mama knew the odds were against the child before it was conceived.
A child conceived to satisfy selfish needs.

Promiscuity is not an athletic game.
It is a sin where we share the wrong thing.

VD is spreading at an epidemic pace.
Another twenty years and we will lose this race.

Even the sophisticated lady got a bug.
You can't get these diseases from hugs.

Yes you are wrong
Without you these problems can't go on.

Emptiness

There is emptiness all around and throughout society.
Empty compassion and empty love has created a world of "no mercy".

Empty purpose and empty opportunity will create "no motivation".
Apathy is an emptiness that will kill people and destroy a nation.

Empty words will devalue anything a body has to say.
Vain behaviors desensitize and turn emergencies into play.

When seriousness goes, vanity has sent it away.
When chaos comes, vanity causes it to stay.

Charity is driven by "what's in it for me?"
Earthly rewards are the motivation for "thank you" and "please."

A vain touch never really touches the sensitive skin.
Vain hugs miss the body and goes straight for the chin.

The Sunday school teacher makes a vain attempt at teaching the cross.
The minister's vain attempt save not, but increases the loss.

Shallow words are spoken with the intention to deceive.
Vanity has left a world with nothing in which to believe.

Love, now comes with many strings attached.
It teases and pulls the victim to a place where he will never come back.

Empty love is a tool of deception that condemns the world.
It has moved from the adult all the way down to the pre-teen boys and girls.

"I love you" means I love what you can do for me.
Lustful pleasure destroys the adult but the children never see.

The façade of the vain world does not expose the abuse our lives take.
The children never see the truth until it makes the same mistake.

The unwed mother breeds more unwed mothers.
And the bastard fathers of the bastard children call each other brothers.

Brother is an empty word that is used as merciless bait.
The word covers the eyes of the victim while the thief takes.

Sister is another empty word used primarily by the man.
Man's use of sister has no gentile love because it is part of a devious plan.

The empty words represent the empty hearts.
Man's life is vain because he has no time for God.

In a world of vanity can you believe anything spoken or written?
The motive is always suspected because the truth is hidden.

A man will call himself a Democrat or Republican because of one agenda item.
He blindly follows vain concepts that are design to mislead him.

There is no substance there, but he will never know it.
The misguided fool is caught up in chaos, and he cannot quit.

It is all vanity that cannot be righted without righteousness.
We selfish humans should learn to care more, not care less.

Doing what is right in the eyes of God is the only way to eliminate vanity.
A true believer is full of the Holy Spirit; therefore his life is not empty.

Are profane words typically spoken by empty children or men with problems?
An ignorant child is ageless because vanity has extended him.

Fifteen-year old boys don't need a belt because the belt line is below the buttocks.
He can never fall because his parents and a drug- dependent society prop him up.

Twelve- year- old girls are made to look like sexy beauty queens and sent out on dates.
They look like half-naked fashion models on a catwalk or harlots on the make.

Vanity - it is all Vanity!

European's Rules

The Whites run away
The Blacks run too

The Whites move from
The Blacks move to

Give and take, take and give
Where does acceptance live?

One moves in, the other moves out
Segregation is what this is about

My school, your school
The professor and the fool

Accept only one kind
Build a city and draw a line

Your church, my cathedral
Same god, different people

I'm first; you are last
Everything has a class

The poor versus the rich
The lady versus the bitch

I am quiet, he's noisy
I talk, he listens to me

The colonist is right
The savage is wrong

Where is God?
What God?

You carry the cross
You also carry the gun

I carry no cross
You also carry the gun

I carry no cross
But I have a spear

You are in my house
You are master; me, slave

You try to make me holy
Listen to yourself talk

I've been wrong for 2000 years
You've been right for 100 years

I had no Sodom till you came
You have sodomized everything

Can you fear God and kill his children?
Is that saving or destroying souls for men?

You eulogize me while I live
You want my land an anything I can give

You use my women and pass them on
Your greed has done irreparable harm

My daughter satisfies your need
She's tainted with the European seed

You took over and told me where to go
Force me off my lands with a decisive blow

You need room in spite of the cost
You must be captain, master or boss

You even conquered the Holy Land
With no Bible but swords in both hands

China has over a billion humans
You still took their land

You right no wrongs
These are the privileges of the strong

What goes around will never come around
You control all coming and going

Much blood on your hands
Nobody knows because you write the books

You look like a god
You think like a god

You tell me you are superior
You tell me I am inferior

You demand the respect of God
Look like, talk like, walk like-

You know the story
You wrote the book

You need no menu
You are chief cook

You make me ugly
You are beautiful

Your women are gentle
My women are rough
Your women are fragile
My women are tough

Your women show tender love
My women have no emotion

Your women can be sexually satisfied
My women are insatiable

Your women are ladylike
My women are trashy

Your women show emotion
My women are emotionless

I like your women the best
You make my women sex slaves

You have functional families
I have dysfunctional families

Native Americans had 1000's of year's head start.
Native Americans are 1000's of years behind

You do wrong to satisfy your greed
You say tomorrow is reserved for right

These are your rules of advantage
The rules change each day
Rules of exploitation are not designed for fair play.

XI Freedom

The freedom poems deal with the racial problems of our society. Most of the poems reflect the effect of racism. The collection includes the following:

1. **Let's Suppose**
2. **Liberty**
3. **Indigenous Music**
4. **Retribution**
5. **Selfish Freedom**
6. **The Black Forest**
7. **The Education of a Slave**
8. **The Euphoric Mind**
9. **The Missing Sound**
10. **The Motivation of the Slave**
11. **The Other Day**
12. **The Pursuit of Happiness**
13. **We Did Not Sing Our Father's Song**
14. **Another Name**
15. **The Black Face**
16. **De dawgs**
17. **The Doomed Slave Chases the Elusive Freedom**
18. **Selfish Sight**
19. **Soft and Fluffy**
20. **Sensitivity**

Let's Suppose

Let's suppose everybody is not equal.
Let's suppose God gave everybody their own land.

Let's suppose you can't stand these inferior folks.
Stop! Now! And take a look at the rights of man.

Let's suppose they appear weak and naïve.
Let's suppose the devil introduced you to greed.

Let's suppose you wanted that big name and big castle.
Then you will exploit these inferior folks for your needs.

Let's suppose you did this till it became the norm.
Let's suppose you have to justify this godless deed.

Let's suppose your conscious has to be appeased.
Then you barbarized, beastified and villianized the folks for greed.

Let's suppose you don't really oppress because of a threat.
Let's suppose you don't conquer because of the need for land.

Let's suppose God asked you for a reason.
How are you going to justify the blood on your hand?

Let's suppose I am inferior to you
Let's suppose you still call me man.

Let's suppose I got my home and you got yours.
Why do you need my inferior children and my land?

Let's suppose you talk about freedom, rights and peace.
Let's suppose you really don't believe these things.

Let's suppose you are pointing your finger at others.
Then you really don't have such a great dream.

Let's suppose you think you are not responsible.
Let's suppose you see wrong but have nothing to say.
Let's suppose it bothers you a little bit.
But a kind word and a smile go a long way.

Liberty

Liberty is lost in the mind
Liberty's womb is the mind

Liberty can grow if there is the will
Liberty is not dead, it lives

But liberty is bound and can't escape
Free your mind before it is too late

Seek liberty while there is time
Liberty will bring peace to your mind

Indigenous Music

Let the music reveal my pain
I am brought down over and over again.

Let the music tell you how I feel
My life is not for real

Let the music reach deep in my soul
The revelation will expose your cold

Let the sad music play on and on
This is no place for a happy song

Play the music so my father can hear
He should know sadness is still here
The moon brings a moan and a tear.

Keep the music slow,
So it can massage your heart
Play for the sad one
Who plays the clown part?

Play slowly for me – play slower for you
Your death for me will take you too.

Retribution

What you looking at me for?
I know what you are thinking.

What you think? I am crazy
Or do you think I been a drinking?

Stop looking at me. Did I do something to you?
Why are you wondering what I'm gonna do?

You got a guilty conscious and it's bothering you.
That's why you are wondering what I am going to do.
What you built up is gonna fall down.
You built on me, I am unstable ground.

That's right! Time doesn't heal these kinds of feelings.
That's why the debt of the father is paid by the children.

You watch me trying to anticipate my plan.
You will only know when it happens because it's in God's hand.

Take a look at yourself, there is evil in you.
You stole my soul and made me evil too.

You teach righteousness and fair play.
But your quest for lucre takes it all away.

What are you-some kind of devil or demon?
You bring misery and death without a conscious.

Don't look at me, you don't have the right.
The inevitable will come in a black draped night.

Selfish Freedom

Freedom in the land of the Free is not what it appears to be.
It is reserved for you, not me.

Freedom is for the special man
The hypocrite with the gun in his hand

He talks love and comes with the cross.
He is free to exploit your body and become your boss.

He preaches fairness and justice and everything good.
Values that were never intended for your neck of the woods.

You are not free to say anything you wish.
That freedom comes with the power to resist.

You are not free to go anywhere you will
Blind ignorance will get you killed.
You are not free to go into some houses of worship.
This rejection is approved by the priest and bishop.

You are not free to live as a man.
It is average people who deny freedom in this land.

Teachers, housewives, preacher, policemen, farmer and chefs
Deny freedom to a Black but demand freedom for self.

Yes! The land of the free is a selfish sort of place.
A land full of hypocrites that will not receive God's grace.

The Black Forest

I stand on a high hill and see black trees struggle for sunlight.
I see restrained life trying to find its way through a perpetual night.

These trees' lost destiny was to become mighty timbers.
Soon the life I see before me will die as coal black embers.
These trees will leave no glory because they have none.
Glory can only be obtained by the motivated exposure to the sun.

They preach stretch, struggle and reach for just a little sunlight.
The never-ending struggle has deformed undeveloped backs.

Never will these trees build a mighty ship or a tiny home.
A life smothered by greatness will watch in agony when opportunity is gone.

What hope has a tree when forced to turn around?
Hope is gone; it died when the sun went down.

A dark world offers only death to a life without hope.
The hopeless is attacked by pestilence, fire and smoke.

A hopeless tree sways with even the slightest winds.
In the storm they fall and never rise again.

The dark forest is full of self-inflicted pain.
The trees suffer from shadow fever and too little rain.

The tall tree tries to cast a shadow over the little brother.
When the light returns the trees will attack each other.

To the big tree every day is a good day.
Only the creator can take the big trees' light away.

The Education of a Slave

Every living thing has some innate capacity to allow it to survive. Even babies react fearfully when the unknown appears to threaten their lives.

To educate is to develop an understanding of the innate manifestations. Man's every actions are based on modifications of capacities that are inborn.

The quest for true education always involves a need to know why. Why this? Why that? Why me? Why you? Why live and why die?

Why does a man need freedom when you can take care of all his needs?
Why not look within yourself for the motivator called greed?

Education is driven by need.
Education is also motivated by greed.

Beyond the basics, education is greatly influenced by opportunity. Why waste time on that which is not a possibility?

Education is first an acknowledgement and secondly a solution. Ones Education will help to locate a relative comfort zone in every trial and tribulation.

What motivates a slave to complete a task; is it fear or reward? Fear may initiate the action but the task is finalized to the criteria of a god.

To satisfy the criterion of God the slave educates himself to do the forced task better.
The slave master does not understand the "comfort zone"; he attributes success to terror.

The slave's efforts were not totally man driven; it eventually came from his heart.

This was only made possible because he was educated about the will of God.

We must mimic the motivation of a slave who contributed in spite of restraining conditions.

To do the best that God expects of us should now become our mission.

Progress requires knowledge to make tomorrow better than today. This concept is not new; this is the key to the success of the educated slave.

Education based on a truth brings improvements in man's attitude and motivation.

Knowledge based on truth will always expose the unacceptable deviations.

If we do not educate each generation about the faults of the past, we will certainly see them in the future.

There is only right and wrong in this world and no one can classify themselves as neutral.

The slave took the best that life offered him and he did what God expected of him.

The slaves' bodies were caught in the grasp of evil but faith, hope and a song freed them.

Today's slaves are those with no knowledge of the truth.
Today's slave efforts are selfish, minimal, chaotic, spontaneous and loose.

To educate man on the peace of the "comfort zone", his heart must lead the way.
There is no selfishness in a divinely inspired heart because compassion rules the day.

True education then and now is to understand that we are to do everything as well as God expects us to do.

The knowledge of the slave's success in trial and tribulation is sent as an example to you.

You are expected to do the best that you can do even when there is a negative support system.

The slave had no choice in his bondage, but when you realize all the efforts that created your greatness you will also realize you owe him.

The Euphoric Mind

In a land of a million blessings, why is reality so hard to accept?
People in this land hide from everything including self.

What's wrong when so many people find safety in an imaginary world?
In an imaginary world everything is false, especially hope and love.

Perhaps it is because so many lack the sense to see the deception.
It is the other person's accomplishment that provides the motivation.

We think what we see and our imagination fills in the rest.
We want what others have because it is desired and accepted by the masses.

An imaginary world offers a false feeling of confidence and happiness. If feelings are false then all perceptions are based on a state of semi-consciousness.

Semi-consciousness means the person is ignorant of his surroundings. Ordinary quickness and keenness of mind is lacking.

In other words, this imaginary world is a state of stupidity.
Can you imagine someone wanting to be less than their best?
To want to be in an imaginary world means that there is a malfunction.
Hiding from reality is a brain disorder that is not a wholesome condition.

Any person who wants to live in a world of make-believe security is stupid.
The person is mentally dull, foolish, senseless or just plain stupid.

Stupidity is a hidden part of the person and can only come out through their actions.

Can you visualize anyone voluntarily entering the stupid world of deceptions?

Taking something to kill the pain may hide the critical alarm.
False security leads to complacency which allows a greater harm.

Once the decay starts it takes immediate action to stop the deterioration.
The euphoria that is the result of chemical stimuli can be deception.

Chemically derived euphoria is today's easy access to the land of deception.

To cut off the effectiveness of the brain is comparable to self-mutilation.

To lessen the mental activity is also distorting right and wrong. The right of the euphoric mind falls in the sphere of the pleasure syndrome.

This unreal world has replaced agape love with self-gratification. It does not matter how a person gets here, it is called the state of intoxication.

Some call this state "under the influence", but a better term would be "out of control."

This is the drunken state where man will certainly lose his soul.

In the imaginary world of good feelings, even the pains of death feel good.
In a drunken state, complex human interactions of love/hate are misunderstood.

Some wrong decisions made "under the influence" cannot be righted in a lifetime of trying.

The wrongful decision that hurts the fellow human will flash before the dying.

People use many drugs to brainwash themselves into believing that wrong is right.

It is easy to cross over into the world of stupidity and go back.

Alcohol is probably the oldest destructive vehicle used for crossing into darkness.
The spirit of God cannot work with a fool's mind because it is senseless.

Imagine the Holy Spirit trying to instruct a person who has his consciousness impaired.
A person under the influence may or may not care if his life is spared.

The purpose for the alcohol and drugs is to produce a controlled behavioral change.
Trying to control the mind by somehow disabling the mind is very strange.

The mind cannot protect the body when it is partially disabled.
When the wisdom of the mind is disabled, the sin of the flesh is enabled.

"For the flesh lusteth against the spirit, and the Spirit against the flesh: and these are contrary the one to the other: so that ye cannot do the things that ye would" (Galatians 5:17.)

The Spirit instructs man through man's mind, if the mind is stupefied, it cannot hear.
Why man let narcotics blunt their senses and create confusion or stupor is not clear.

I Thessalonians 5:19 has a key directive in it.
Drugs and alcohol in every case will quench the Spirit.

Illegitimate babies are born because a stupefied person cannot love.
The taboo against fornication cannot be communicated from above.

The spirit is trying to communicate that this act is wrong.
This is why so many sex scared babies are born.

Drugs prevent the spirit from stopping the slaughter of men.
It is drugs and alcohol that cause the violent disputes between friends.

It is in the state of stupid stupor where most illegitimate babies are born.
Under the influence of deadly narcotics, man will kill, steal and bring great harm.

A drug crazed mind cannot control even the simple thing it believes.
This crippled mind feels that it can touch things it does not see.

Under the influence, no becomes yes and yes becomes no.
Even danger is answered in the affirmative, never shadowed by "I think so".

Reason is replaced by an impulsive drive for pleasure.
Live and be happy takes away any fear of failure.

Agape love is replaced by Eros or better yet lust.
Fellow humans are forced to be last while self is first.

Children's first exposure is the imaginary world of stupid men.
They are attracted by the lies and trapped long before reality set in.

Stupidity stands out because it raises a flag and wants to be seen.
Children learn without reason because their mind is still green.

A green basket left uncovered will collect apathetic men's trash.
They will conveniently deposit their rubbish as long as the empty space last.

Therefore, men with mental deficiencies create children with impaired judgment.
When a child sees what the parent does, then he is a product of the environment.

The standards are set by men who are less than their best.
A child exposed to a drug and alcohol crazed society will fail the test.

Drugs and alcohol bring with them all the forbidden sins.
Pleasure and vain pride are the only things that matter to the captured men.

Prisoner of a war that is bad, and soon to be lost.
They feel no pain; therefore they will never know the cost.

Their children die but they can only cry dry tears.
Their daughters become women years before their years.

Their sons will never marry because fidelity has never been seen.
If every day is a dream world, then there is no time or place to dream.

Why deal with reality when a little pill will erase yesterday and tomorrow.
Take a drink when you don't want to know what you need to know.

Drugs are an anti-ambition medicine; it will take away the need to be employed.
Alcohol and a 9 millimeter gun will guarantee that you will not be scared.

Cocaine is an anti-aid drug that also works against other STDs.
Marijuana will make you invisible so that you can take whatever you need.

Drugs are like the darkness and will hide you as you abuse a child.
You can beat a man to death and for each blow a satisfying smile.

You can tear down your own neighborhood and blame it on somebody else.
You will urinate on the wall; write on the walls just to show them that you don't care.

You will tear down public housing and say they should do better by you.
You will turn down the low paying job and complain that you don't have anything to do.

You do not understand this is what a drug and alcohol infested environment will do.
You are no longer a man; you are a shell of what God had planned for you.
You will try to place blame on others, but never on the power you take.
God gave you the brain to take you places but the decision is yours to make.

The body is a creation of God; it can heal many of the deep pains.
It is foolish to inhibit the healing process by disabling the brain.

Drugs and alcohol are everywhere and have brought this world much death.
The dope fiend and alcoholics cannot love his brother because he does not love himself.

He can make babies but he will throw them away.
He cannot see tomorrow because he lives from day to day.

His ghetto is a ghetto because he operates with part of a brain.
He has created so many fatherless babies he does not know their name.

His woman is worst than him and doesn't care who knows it.
She will bare half-brothers and half-sisters until time or death make her quit.

Half is a fitting description for people who operate with half a brain.
Generation after generation will make the same mistake over and over again.

They don't consider God in any of the pleasure seeking things they do.
They are Godless Christians who are the worst kind of hypocrites too.

They make no genuine attempt to love God and their neighbor.
Their covetous eyes are looking for any opportunity to score.

They will rape the babies' body and take the babies food.
Their hearts of stone, pumps drug tainted cold, colorless blood.

A person in a state of stupidity cannot make the correct decisions.
Temporary stupidity has produced an overflow of loveless conceptions.

A young girl makes a decision based on ignorance to get stupid before she crosses over into womanhood.
She does not realize that she has been disabled, and she will be exploited because her sense cannot separate bad from good.

A child born from self-imposed stupidity is no accident or a mistake.
Imperfections and failures are the result of some devious plan or the chances we take.

People do not become addicted to outside stimuli; it is the inward stupidity we crave.
Stupidity conceals the fear of the future and the demons of the past, it erases.

Stupid people walk around without a concern or care.
To them everything is going to be alright because they have no fear.

The stimuli erases the fear and the beefed up pleasure zone replaces it.
The infected world starts to crumble, which the power of half a brain cannot fix.

The euphoric mind says, "I am not a murderer because I did not kill". If you surround a child with death; he will die before his time because of your will.

Stupidity's weapons of choice are the absence of love, negligence and apathy.
Most of the children on welfare have a father who cannot or will not provide basic necessities.

The euphoric mind tells the girl and woman she is not a prostitute because she did not accept money.
Many sell their bodies for a few words of praise, like "you are a good looking honey."

To a woman in a stupor, pleasure moves to the top of her list.
Her dress, talk and walk are all indicators of her main wish.

If she feel good about herself normally, then that feeling become action in a stupor.
Even the quite shy ones become an overt pleasure seeker when you drug her.
A mother becomes a step-mother when she drugs herself.
The motherly qualities step-down the moment she relinquishes control to something else.

Some foolish women take drug and alcohol before their babies are born.
They do this with clear knowledge the long term effect and proven harm.

A fool is a stupid person who lacks judgment or sense.
Foolishness comes with alcohol and drug dependence.

If a person does foolish things, they are at best temporarily foolish.
The permanent damage and scars are on par with a "death wish".

The foolish act may involve injecting, snorting, drinking, smoking, and taking a pill.
A vast variety of drugs are used to satisfy the physical and psychological will.

The drug abuser describe their indulgence as "getting high" or "messing up their mind"
A better description would be "killing me gently with time" and "stupidly blind"

The Missing Sound

People die because they hear no sound.
People cry because they hear no sound.
People are lost because they hear no sound.

The African drums beat no more
A lost race has no place to go.

A confused people with no direction no goals
The lost drums took their souls.

People die because they hear no sound.
People cry because they hear no sound.
People lost because they hear no sound.

The African drum must come again.
The sound of the drum can revive these lost men.

This is the missing reference that goes deep.
Our Shallow references are why we sleep.

The Motivation of a Slave

Every living thing has some innate capacity to allow it to survive. Even babies react fearfully when the unknown appears to threaten their lives.

To educate is to develop an understanding of the innate manifestations. Man's every actions are based on modifications of capacities that are inborn.

The quest for true education always involves a need to know why. Why this? Why that? Why me? Why you? Why live and why die?

Why does a man need freedom when you can take care of all his needs?
Why not look within yourself for the motivator called greed?

Education is driven by need.
Education is also motivated by greed.

Beyond the basics, education is greatly influenced by opportunity. Why waste time on that which is not a possibility?

Education is first an acknowledgement and secondly a solution. Ones Education will help to locate a relative comfort zone in every trial and tribulation.

What motivates a slave to complete a task, fear or reward?
Fear may initiate the action but the task is finalized to the criteria of God.

To satisfy the criterion of God the slave educates himself to do the forced task better.
The slave master does not understand “comfort zone”; he attributes success to terror.

The slave’s efforts were not totally man driven; it eventually came from his heart.
This was only made possible because he was educated about the will of God.

We must mimic the motivation of a slave who contributed in spite of restrained conditions.
To do the best that God expects of us should now become our mission.

Progress requires knowledge to make tomorrow better than today.
This concept is not new; this is the key to the success of the educated slave.

Education based on a truth brings improvements in man’s attitude and motivation.
Knowledge based on truth will always expose the unacceptable deviations.

If we do not educate each generation about the faults of the past, we will certainly see them in the future.
There is only right and wrong in this world and no one can classify themselves as neutral.

The slave took the best that life offered him and he did what God expected of him.
The slaves’ bodies were caught in the throng of evil but faith, hope and a song freed them.

Today's slaves are those with no knowledge of the truth.
Today's slave efforts are selfish, minimal, chaotic, spontaneous and loose.

To educate man on the peace of the "comfort zone", his heart must lead the way.
There is no selfishness in a divinely inspired heart because compassion rules the day.

True education then and now is to understand that we are to do everything as well as God expects us to do.
The knowledge of the slave's success in trial and tribulation is sent as an example to you.

You are expected to do the best that you can do even when there is a negative support system.
The slave had no choice in his bondage, but when you realize the causes of your greatness you will also realize you owe him.

The Other Day

A defeated African prisoner once said,
"There's gonna be another day"

This tormented soul came out of the
Dark hole of a slave ship and said,
"There's gonna be another day"

A beaten and tortured field hand said,
"There's going to be another day"

The African dies a slave death but
His last words were meant to be

Hope for those left behind
"There's gonna be another day"

"There's gonna be another day"
Became the pacifier for many generations
Of slaves and all who followed.

The day is here. Make it right
For all those who used the phrase
To appease a captured soul.

There is not time to waste.
Millions of tormented souls wanted
This day for you, to make amends
For the pains of the lost souls.

The Pursuit of Happiness

The pursuit of happiness is the endeavor for which we live.
If your happiness comes at the expense of my happiness,
Your happiness is not real.

If your fellowman is truly happy then so will you.
Take his hand in peace and love, and happiness will come too.

We Did Not Sing our Father's Song

Let us express our appreciation to our Lord in a song.
Let us sing about our trials, tribulations and the troubles he has brought us from.

We cannot sing in **harmony** unless we are in agreement in feeling or opinion.
How can a **liberated** people remain free if they forget those who inspired freedom?

Our voice should project a confident belief in God's truth and permeate the world in profoundness.
We have the opportunity to sing because someone gave their all and others their best.

We shall sing this song with a fervor that says thank you for this exultant happiness.
Because God has worked in the **past** to give me the right and power to act, believe and express.

We are where we are by the grace of God; therefore, by faith we are confident our expectation will be fulfilled.
We must come together as a loving people before we reach the final hill.

Our struggle has been long and hard but we still have many trials to come.
We have fallen into a crevasse of selfishness that is controlled by the evil one.

Our **road** was once paved with **stones** but we have taken the wrong road filled with boulders
There is no **victory** for a people who do not respect and love each other.

The **chastening rod** brings **bitter** sorrow because it is passed from the slave owner to the brother.
Our **hope** is shackled in a quagmire and we have no place to anchor.

We still laggardly move in retrogression to a **steady beat**.
The deceptive euphoria of the moment does not bring **weariness** to our **feet**.

We have come to the place which to our fathers was a tormented longing.
Through the muddy **tears** and the **bloody tracks**, we move without even trying.

We are stuck in reverse and the **gloomy past** is set to overwhelm our **bright star**.
The God of our fathers' weary year has tolerated and protected us **thus far**.

Our God, such a good God has showed us the **way**, and showed us the **light**.
Sometimes I don't understand why it is so hard for man to do right.

We are off the God directed path because we are too **drunk** to pray.
The **wine of the world** has caused our feet to stray too far away.

But, what about the children, will they ever understand?
Who is going to tell them their Golden Future has been broken by the greed of man?

Another Name

Where are we going now that the train is here?
Where are we going now that prosperity has arrived?
Why is the path beyond prosperity so unclear?
Three generations lost while the confused decide.

Which direction to take now that we are free.
No Moses to step forward to lead a liberated man.
Among the masters, freedom is not meant to be.
How can freedom come when power?
Remains in the master's hand?

The Black Face

The deep dark lines cut through a gentle face.
The bottomless furrows reflect the anguish of a race.

Dark eyes that no longer contrast the skin
Tells a sorrowful tale of where this soul has been.

A mournful smile that brings sympathetic pain
A futile face that has no name

Sparse enamel that is brown with age
Lips that smile to cover the rage

Hair that is black, white and brown
A sun baked forehead with a permanent frown

I feel pity for there is pity there.
This soul has an enormous burden to bear.

Oh where is love? Where is family? Where are friends?
Neglect sleep where hope has never been.

The lines tells how this life flowed
A stymied life with no room or time to grow.

Crow's-feet caused by too much strain and sun.
The lean dimpled face of a man forced to run.

A stately chin with a distinguished cleft
Exalted in exploitation, now waits on death.

De Dawgs

De dawgs da be a comin; da be a comin fast
I tide now; I don't know if-in my strength will las

I ben ah run-in seem like be fo days
I ain't bother no-body, but they be takin my freedom away.

I is tied but I want-ta be free.
I do dis run-in fo freedom, but the master sick the dawgs on me.

Free-dom war you be
Free-dom war you be

Da tell me out thar is a riv-a I got-to cross.
De dawgs da be a gain-in, and I is fraid it's loss.

O----oh free-dom! war you be.
O----oh freedom! save po me.

I got to find a riv-a, a riv-a is all I be need-in
Can't hold out much longer, I is tied and be a bleed-in.

De dawgs day be close now, like day upon me.
I got-ta find dat riv-a, I –sa got-ta cross.

O----oh free-dom! where you be
O-----oh free-dom! come hair to me.
Oh, my Lord, where is dat riv-a

I best b runn-in with all that I can

Da done bought my chillum, now I be lone.
Lord! Sho me dat water that I can walk on.

Lord! Tis old nu and I just want to taste dis sher free-dom.
Hep! Po me Father, I is tied and de dawgs day come.

O---oh! Lord! hav mercy on me.
O---oh! Lord! I just wanna be free.

O----oh free-dom! Where do you be?
O---oh free-dom de dawgs soon be on me.

Wa-ter! Wa-ter! I hear de wa-ter come fo me
I be clos now, soon I be free.
Thar da river lay-in dere b-fo me.
But a riv-er to big to make me free.
Lord! I can't swim an I-is scad of de wa-ter dat black.
Mi free-dom is on de other side and I can't turn back.

De dawgs be a-com-in I can hair dem thru da trees.
De riv-er to wide to cross; I suppose to die here on my nees.

Mi life don ben a budon and mi only only footprint is in sand.
Damarrow I be a dead slave or I be a free man.

Dar iv-er is a flooded and de wat-er much too fast and hi.
I rat-er float to he-ben than live and die.

I be dead as I live, Lord! I be mighty dead.
You sho me Your free-dom; now, I no longer fraid.

De riv-er! she be high, way bove mi head.
I am just to walk across; cause I ain't fraid.

De dawg be close; I hear dare tounge lap at the leves.
I is gonna walk cross dis deep river caus I wan-ta be free.

I have no more fear of what dis wold can do to mi.
I will walk dis wa-ter caus damorrow I will be free.

O---oh free-dom hair I come; O---oh free-dom it is mi.
I thank mi wonderful God! He do made mi free.

If-in da bossman could see mi now, she me walk dis black sea.
He would have to feel good to see a man walk on water to be free.

The riv-er deep, the riv-er wide
But I can walk to the other side.

De dawgs hind mi look but the bark be cease.
De dog be trying but day cn't walk dis wa-ter like mi.

De free-dom I look for done come to me at last.
Der joy in my life cause al mi sorrow be past.

De joy on dis swift riv-er, an no fear in sight.
I walk de wa-ter of free-dom; I neber will go back.

One-way to Freedom

I walk the waters of freedom; it cannot be too deep.
I walk the waters of freedom and Jesus waits for me.

My faith in Jesus is whole and I shall get to the other side.
My life has been perfected by the trials and the tears I cry.

I walk the water of freedom and Jesus urge me on.
He said you must follow me, if you want to get home.

I walk the waters of freedom; it cannot be too deep.
I walk the waters of freedom and Jesus waits for me.

My eyes are on Jesus; my faith is complete.
He guides my soul, through His Holy Spirit to eternity.

He took my heart in His hand and molded it to His name.
I stop treading water and my life will never be the same.

I walk the waters of freedom; it cannot be too deep.
I walk the waters of freedom and Jesus waits for me.

When He came into my life I began to see the other bank.
As long as my eyes remain on Jesus, I don't have time to sink.

One day I will touch His wonderful hand, then I'll know I made it across.
If it wasn't for the cross, I would surly been among the lost.

I walk the waters of freedom; it cannot be too deep.
I walk the waters of freedom and Jesus waits for me.

The doomed Slave chases the Elusive Freedom

I ben running for de river for three days.
The dogs be a coming to take what I don't have away.

De briars done toe my clothes and toe up my feet.
De dogs ben so hot at me I ain't had time to eat.

I had to run caus I wants to be free.
I tried to find my woman and chillum but time done run out on me.

De master, he done sold em to da nu master.
I don't know where she be but I be looking for her.

Thay say Master Tate brought my women and my chillum.
I been running three days trying to find thum.

Now I go-na set on dis river bank and let them catch me.
I 's tired, I can't run no mo, I is too tired to be free.

Where is de freedom in dis land of de free?
Why de God let em make a slave O me?

Oh! Freedom where you be?
Is it freedom dat take my folks from me?

Oh! Freedom where do you hide?
Freedom you went when you sold my wife?

Oh! Freedom dis river is too big to cross.
Here I'll die because all is lost.

Come Master the ol'e boy can't run no moe.
Come dogs, my mind is weary and my body sore.

I is ready to be taken, I is ready to go home.
Oh freedom! Oh freedom! Oh freedom!

Selfish Sight

Let me see for myself, I know what is real.
I don't trust your eyes, they tell me how you feel.
I can see for myself and I can see wrong and right.
Your eyes will destabilize me and keep me off track

I can see the world in an untainted spectrum.
Your version is self-serving and designed to lead me on.

Give me time and space to let me see what I must.
Doubt and anxiety come from eyes I don't trust.

Let me use my eyes and my mind to try to understand.
If God did not want differences He would have
given eyes and mind to only one man.

Soft and Fluffy

A soft fluffy substance that has brought hardness to so many
It represents misery because it brought innocent souls plenty.

Its soft touch pricks the careless hand.
It represents both a blessing and a curse to man.

Its weight is scattered around the hill.
The weight of gold when the sacks are filled

The old and the young crawl among the weeds with sacks to fill
The privileged stand and watch from a distant hill.

This job will last a lifetime because the rows never end.
This is a terrible destiny that was contrived by men.

The future for these souls is exactly like the past.
Each generation will follow the row for as long as their lives lasts.

But the row will go on and on until the end of time.
The row is passed to all generations because it is in their mind.

The softness will never bring the comfort that they anticipate.
The way out is almost gone, I fear, they have waited too late.

Generation after generation feel the pull of a full sack.
The power of the greed is holding all the generations back.

Hope has been replaced by a temporary comfort zone.
When age moves in then comfort moves on.

The child and the adult learn to accept less in a land of plenty.
Dreams are the only way out but the dream will kill many.

The future offers weekend rest and Saturday night good times.
Generation after generation of night people with moonshine on their mind

People who play house, church, community, and mom and dad are everywhere.

The soft fluffy substance has produced a multitude of people who don't care.

They don't care about life, children, liberty or heaven.
All their hope rides on the numbers, seven and eleven.

The soft fluffy substance had damaged a people all the way to its soul.
They don't think or plan any more, they just do what they are told.

The world doesn't care about them and they don't care about themselves.
They live for today and eagerly wait on death.

Death will come quickly and it will not be soft.
How do you save millions of people who enjoy being lost?

Sensitivity

You enslave me, made fun of me, oppress me.
Now you question my sensitivity.

You Damn Right I Am Sensitive

You lynch me, you beat me, you imprison me
You tried to dehumanize me

You Question My Sensitivity
You despised me, you took my children, you took my woman.
You did not take my soul.

Come on! You Question My Sensitivity

You terrorized me, you made me feel inferior

You made me think I am ugly.
Now! You Question My Sensitivity

You call me stupid, you say I can't learn
You segregate me.

You Don't Understand Sensitivity

You have modified my behavior.
I have learned to be wary of you
Under these conditions you would be sensitive too.

You were Lawless in a society with Rules.
In your game I played the part of the Fool.

I Am Confused – Just What Are You.

You worship a God but do the devil's deeds.
You are incapable of love, your motivation is Greed.

I Am Sensitive To You, You have NO Godly Values.
You uphold Freedom and Justice in a selfish way.
You buy slaves, Kill, Father Half Black Bastards and
Still find time to pray.

Why Should I Not Be Sensitive.

You paint everybody as a savage but yourself a saint.
My sensitivities are there
I've been trained to look for the negative.
You brought pain from everywhere.

I've been slapped by a weak man to prove my inferiority.

I've been kicked to show my powerlessness.
I've been hanged to terrorize me.
I've been burned to keep me in my place.
I've been castrated to take away my masculinity.
I've been called names to make me sub-human.
I've been made fun of to demoralize me.

You call me a coward because I ran when twenty men attacked me.
You have never taken me one on one with equal footing
So who is the coward?

Yes! I Am Sensitive, This Is Learned Behavior

XII Hodgepodge

This section contains a mixture of poetic concepts:

1. **As Long**
2. **Baby Love Is Forever**
3. **Conscience**
4. **Don't You Know**
5. **Hope and an Idea**
6. **Life**
7. **Morning**
8. **Better**
9. **Your Heart Is Your Face**
10. **Truth and Anguish**
11. **War**
12. **Warm Blood**

As Long

As long as we live we need to grow.
We can't live long when held down low.

As long as we walk, let's walk with pride.
Please! Don't look down, don't run and don't hide.

As long as we breathe, breathe deep and long.
Enjoy this free air, it will soon be gone.

As long as we eat, let's eat to stay alive.
Without good food, how long will you survive?

As long as we have to sleep, sleep well.
A two-ended candle leads to a living hell.

As long as we are to produce, do the best you can.
The ability to gauge and change is unique to man.

As long as we love, let's love with all our heart.
This role demands love, whether you play the male or female part.

As long as we are here, let's do our very best.
This is a temporary place, it is God's test.

Baby Love is Forever

I was a baby once with needs a-plenty.
I needed hands to support me and God sent me many.

I needed love and a bosom much warmer than a womb.
I needed protection from Beelzebub's doom.

I needed a strong hand to guide me through this perilous life.
That kind of strength only comes when husband merges with wife.

I learned to crawl, I learned to walk and I learned to run.
I knew as an infant, I had much to do before I was done.

But I had needs that went beyond wants and everybody knew it.
There I was a helpless baby with nothing of my own to survive with.

Look at me now, all grown up on what you fed me.
If you don't like what you see, then who is guilty?

Yes! I was an ignorant child who knew nothing.
All that I am now came from learned things.

If you didn't want me to sin, why expose me to a sinful environment.
My exposure came very early and remained throughout my life with
yearly
installments.

I am what you wanted me to be and taught me to be.
The idle mind will be filled with either good or bad deeds.

Influence will come; there is no way to stop it.
God's law is designed to expose good and control it.

Look at a once empty vessel now filled with your permissiveness
Death and destruction follows a vessel when corruption fills them.

I can't be at fault because you taught me everything I know.
You protected me from the obvious but it is society that has delivered
the deathblow.

Don't weep for me, save your tears for yourself.
I die quickly but your whole life will be a slow death.

Examine your world; is it safe to bring up the innocent and ignorant?
A child dies before it is born; this is as corrupt as it gets.

Conscience

A conscience that allow one to steal
will also allow that one kill.

The conscience that promote a lie
is the same consciousness that urges getting high?

A conscience that permits minor wrong is
Also capable of producing major harm

Any deviant conscience that is allowed to tarnish a name
can only bring death and destruction to man

A conscience starts out weak and grows strong
how the conscience is nurtured determines right or wrong

A conscience that does not restrain allows chaos to prevail.
This type conscience is bound for hell.

"Don't You Know?"

When one is asked "Don't you know?"
You wonder what you don't know.

Seek the right person to find what you don't know
Just remember that I told you so.

Quit trying to understand "what" and "what for"
Try to understand "Don't you know."

When you have wasted all your time and still "Don't you know"
Then it is time to talk to "Who-do-know."

"Who-do-know" can tell you "what for" and why "Don't you know"
"Who-do-know" is always called "sho-nuff-Jo."

If you got a problem and just "Don't you know"
Take the little ole problem to "sho-nuff- Jo."

"sho-nuff-Jo" can tell you everything that you need to know
The "whys", "what is", "what's happening", "what gives", and "what for" of
"Don't you know?"

Hope and an Idea

Why does my heart flutter when I hear "God Bless America"?

Is it the fact or the idea?

Why does my emotion run so high when I sang "The
Star Spangled Banner"?

Is it the freedom or the idea?

Why do I feel included when I hear or sing the songs?
Is it really the inclusion or the exclusion that elevates my emotion?

Maybe there is something about the noble idea that make
Me hope for one hundred percent inclusion.

Yes it has got to be the "Hope and the Idea" that bring
The goose bumps to my soul, the chills to my body and the tears to my eyes.

Life

Life is dynamic and seeks its' end.
Life breaks easily, it will not bend.

Life thrives on suffering and pain
Life travels in a downward spin.

Life moves too fast to keep under control
In a flash it releases another soul.

Life carries little joy and less happiness.
Life deals out apprehension and duress.

Life is short and waits for no one.
In one moment in time and infant is gone.

Life is full of traps and pitfalls
It is life that lets you down when time calls.

It is life that pulls the trigger
A hard life makes a little stress bigger.

Life will tear your world apart
Life ceases from a broken heart.

Life brings down the elevated
Life demonizes the holy sainted.

Life pulls the foundation from the wall.
Life pushed the home to make it fall.

Life attacks the strong and the children
Life has abandoned the weakened.

I know life and now you do too.
You've been warned now it is up to you.

Grab a hold on life and ride it to the line.
Better start today, you are running out of time.

THIS IS LIFE!!!!!!

Morning

The morning air brings out the best of the land.
The cover of the darkness revived a tired man.

The morning glory knows the morning is the best of time.
Morning people are at their best because of a rewound mind.

The morning sun is not too hot and beautiful to see.
The morning doves fly in pairs above the tall pine tree.

The morning moon is dim now because it has folded up its light.
The moon is usually at its best after midnight.

The morning dog is up early, trying to find something to eat.
The night cat has found the morning the best time to sleep.

The farmer is up at 4 o'clock to take advantage of the cool morning.
He'll plow several acres before the sun starts cooking.

The housewife is up at 5 o'clock making ready the food.
She knows that at 6:30 the children will be off to school.

The factory worker gets to sleep till about 6:00 o'clock.
He has plenty of time to shower, shave and eat before he must be at the loading dock.
The school teacher will make it to the school a half hour before the bell rings.
She spent the prior evening preparing for the morning.

The children are morning children too and are anticipating the day.
To the children the morning recess is the best time to play.

Better

You are getting better
You gotta get better
You are better today
Than you were yesterday.

Are you a better man?
Are you a better fool?
You have gotten better
Without the benefit of school.

You are growing better women and men
You are growing better children.

Think of where you are
Look at where you've been
You've gotten better all right
You are better at sin.

Your heart is Your Face

Others may wonder about you, but I think I know you.
If others knew what I know they would know you too.

God has given each of us the sight to see beneath the surface.
Your heart represents everything about you and it extends to your face.

Your face experience many changes but the most consistent change continues to hold.
In time your facial expression is a reaction that is out of your control.

If your heart is sad your face will display your pain as a frown.
You will seldom smile because your frown will turn your smile up-side-down.
If you have a mean heart your face will be that of an intimidator.
Your mouth will speak the mean words that commonly found in the troublemaker.

Your mouth is part of your face; therefore, it is part of your heart.
Wise and foolish words have one thing in common; it is the heart where they get their start.

That smirk on your lip indicates that you have a mischievous mind.
Your heart will attack only when your prey is blind.

The shifty eyes are hiding something that is a shameful part of you. Correcting and confessing your fault will bring peace to your heart and free you too.

The face of the clown is a mask that covers insecurity. The funny lip and the antics will never end because they will never bring peace.

The stern or stoic face is more pronounce in a carefree situation. The stern requires the order and commitment found in a well run organization.

Truth and Anguish

The pool of life is made from drops of anguish
The pain of deception is the essence of anguish.

We are mislead from our first cogitative encounter
And anguish will follow.

Our first encounter should be the truth
This is the only escape from the anguish.

The truth prevents the anguish
And the truth cures the anguish
But where is the truth?

The truth is held back to make room for pleasure.
Anguish follows pleasure everywhere it goes.

Truth will come if you want it
But only one drop at a time

War

Piercing screams and moans are everywhere.
Fear is boundless in death's lair

Death stands on yonder ridge and counts his prey.
Death shouts in ecstasy, for this is a good day.

The wounded climb to the ridge, pleading for life.
Death's heart is hard, he gives the knife.

Aliens fight face to face all day.
They kill fellow humans without hate or rage.

The victor never questions why men must die.
The vanquished always question, why?

Death celebrates the end of life.
War is death's macabre sacrifice.

No hesitation as the bayonet strikes the heart.
This is war, mercy plays no part.

Twisted bodies with limbs all-around.
Blood fill boot turned upside down.

Eyes that stare permanently into space.
Moans and screams both emanates from this place.

Many entails exposed to the rain.
What's left of a skull is without brains.
A hand still clutching a weapon is lost and alone.

In a field full of blood red bones.
This is war!!!!!

Warm Blood

I got hills to climb before I am gone.
All I need is something to keep me warm.

The road I travel will lead me home.
I got peace because I travel not alone.

Where cometh warmth when I travel alone?
I know I will be alright when I get home.

In the mean time, I got hills to climb before I am gone.
I only appear to the world to be alone.

I don't mind the hills because I am going home
and the blood from the cross will keep me warm

XIII Christian

This list of poem deals with interaction between people that profess to be Christians. The first poem, "Because it is the Spirit within me" was written for a young man who at the time was suffering from terminal cancer. Several poems were written for a benefit presentation for persons with dreaded illnesses. The list of Christian poems includes the following:

1. **Mercy**
2. **Blood**
3. **For Me**
4. **Forgive**
5. **I Don't Care**
6. **I Gave My Best**
7. **Lie**
8. **Nail Scared Hand**
9. **Omni Enemies**
10. **The Sin of the Kin**
11. **The Light of the World**
12. **The Soothing Tears**
13. **The Window**
14. **Two Fist Full of Dust**
15. **Wants and Needs**
16. **Where Is Peace?**
17. **The Birth of the Light**

Mercy?

The creature is a life form of no clemency.
Lower animals kill for food and cannot afford mercy.

Man does not eat man but man kills and cripples man.
The killing of man was never part of the original plan.

The motive for man killing man can be found in the brain.
The animal killing for food is also in the brain but the motive is not the same.

Death among the animals is quick because the kill is supper.
Man is motivated to get even and make someone suffer.

Mercy is a devalued fruit of the Christian spirit.
Man rips a breathing baby out of the womb and kills it.

There is no mercy; this is a kill crazy society.
They kill the dying because man has not learned pity.

Everybody has a gun with the intent of "blowing somebody away".
No set time for killing because it is high-noon every hour of every day.

"Thou shall not kill" means nothing to a kill crazy people.
Now man uses bombs and machine guns because killing is easier.

The tough guy is the tough guy because he supposedly has nerves of steel.
The real tough guy absorbs provocation, turns the other cheek and refuses to kill.

Six days of the week children are taught how to fight and kill man.
A few hours of the week they are taught how to offer a loving hand.

A worldly reputation grows when it follows an evil path.
The spirit filled reputation dies a quick earthly death but only it will last.

The teenager needs to say, "Take a look at me I have arrived".
Most of their environmental influences have been about ruined lives.

So the teenage proof is based on the ills of society and damnation.
To a society who loves death and violence, evil is the only way to attract attention.

Mercy is synonymous with compassion and charity, grace, clemency and forbearance.
Society teaches children to "kick him when he is down," "hit him back," and "don't give him a chance."

This society will not "leave it alone"; this society gets even plus some.
The innocent bystander is written off as the unfortunate one.

Nuke the wife; nuke the child when you only want the man.
If mercy is based on guilt by association, then we are guilty enough to bring the world to an end.

Our God is a merciful God who tolerates our very evil ways.
He knows we do not deserve his grace but he keeps giving us days.

Our heroes are big, bad, cold-blooded killers.
Alexander the Great's accomplishments were extraordinary but he was a murderer.
The bloody terror of television is the creation of a sick society.
Children learn the possibility and then the fiction becomes the reality.

Bludgeoning, decapitation and limb severing are all ways to bleed a body to death.
The children discover a macabre joy in bringing pain to someone else.

Ignorant children see a reason and accept the first answer conceived.
If violence is so accepted then it must be right in making others bleed.

The message is not that the righteous always wins.
The message is that inflicting death and pain is not a sin.

Society is fascinated by brazen courage and ignores the unrighteous deed.
Numbers are sensationalized by tall tales of how much and how many were made to bleed.

The person in the safe-zone has no mercy for the vanquished enemy.
The weak are at the strong's mercy and the weak are many.

The illegitimate child is the product of a father who knows no mercy.
Unlike the abortionist, they kill slowly and torture us by denying basic necessities.

Where there is no mercy there is no love.
A merciless society has made this a very cruel world.

The unmerciful people will grow old and helpless one day.
The lack of mercy they nurtured will take advantage of their helpless state.

The old are cast aside and left to rot in a small room of their own.
Some are unmercifully shipped to a place of wheel chairs called the "old folks home."

It is possible unmerciful recycles or recreates itself.
The lack of mercy helps fill the "old folk's homes", but it also helps fill the daycares.

It is unkind to separate a young child from his/her mother.
Daycare is the "young folk's home" for the young victims of the unmerciful.
Those who support "day care" will one day support "dependent care".
Those who fill the "day care" will one day fill "dependent care" facilities.
Those who put their children in "day care" will be put in "dependent care".
facilities.
The parent will be fed the same unmerciful that was given to the babies.
The lack of mercy is a sign that man is in deep trouble.

Blood

The key to eternity is the fluid that sustains me.
The fluid of life broke my chains and set me free.

The fluid opened my blind eyes and now I can see true peace.
This life sustaining liquid also exposed the truth to me.

This wonderful substance was given to all free of cost.
Without the life sustaining blood, the body is lost.

Yes! The blood is the fluid that has done more than sustain me.
The blood broke my bonds and brought me true peace.

A celestial transfusion has purified my soul and set me free.
I am on the right road now and nothing, nothing can divert me.

Oh, the blood, such a wonderful gift to receive.
I am now a full-blooded follower of my benefactor's lead.

My blood is pure, my mission defined, and my heart is right.
I am going full speed ahead, and never will I go back.

A full-blooded soul will stay on the right trail.
The full-blooded soul is destined to never fail.

The fluid brings me joy and my continence shows it.
I got joy and peace and I like to share it.

Oh the blood, that wonderful life-giving blood has filled me to the top.
I am a full-blooded soul, now my work will not stop.

I am full-blooded; nothing about me is fractional at all.
I got my transfusion by answering my Benefactor's call.
A full-blooded person will know his way home.
They seeks the lost, to take the lost along.

The transfusion exposes the full-blooded commission.
They are prepared for the future but not the present rejection.

The full-blooded must continue to try in spite of the negative gain.
A full-blooded Noah had only eight positives to claim.

Yes! I am full-blooded and my future is set in stone.
But, I am sad because I can't seem to bring others along.

I am truly troubled because rejection is a form of pain.
But there is hope that I have made unseen gains.

I am full-blooded Christian who realizes life's ups and downs.
The sins of the world are a wall that a Christian must go around.

A soul full of blood will still push to save the lost.
This is the priority directive that came from the cross.

I am a full of blood and anxious to share it with others.
I would like to make all of mankind my full-blooded brother.

You see, it is in the blood where love flows.
A simple transfusion is all that is needed to let love grow.

For Me

My Jesus died on the cross – he died for me
My Jesus died on a cross so I could be free.

My Jesus hung there for hours and he suffered much pain
He gave his life to wash away my sins.

His blood flowed freely and was warm to the touch
My Jesus gave his life because he loved me so much.

That day the lighting flashed and the thunder rolled.
He gave his all for my undeserving soul.

The sun dimmed and the world grew dark
This was a tragic day – man killed God.

Forgive

Forgive is a lonely word that should not stand alone
Forgive is a temporary fix for a troubled mind
But forgiveness can repair a broken home
And it can also leave the past behind

To forgive is not just to excuse
To forgive is not just to pardon
To excuse does not wipe out the abuse
To pardon is to leave it alone

To truly forgive is to disremember or clear the mind
The injured party has no control of his memory
The perpetrator has control of the forgivable line
Forgiveness alone only brings on deep mental misery

So if you want to be forgiven or excused,
Somebody is going to have to accept and forget
To simply say "forgive me" breaks this rule
Only honest explanations can bury the hatchet

I Don't Care!

Morality and love are gone and I know not where.
I come to tell you they have been replaced by "I don't care".

Honor for father and mother and obedience is no longer here.
Righteousness is now bound by "I don't care".

"I don't care" wipes out trust and concern for others.
Everybody practice "I don't care", even Christian mothers.

If the parent doesn't care, then the children's "I don't care" are amplified.
A child born in an "I don't care" world will find it hard to survive.

The mother doesn't care about the child.
She cares too much about the latest style.

The father doesn't care about the home.
The father chases pleasure until his time is gone.

If we don't care, how can bad situations get better?
Human problems are here because we do not care about others.

Do we really care about what tomorrow may bring?
In a land of plenty who needs to dream?

So why care or worry about the deficiencies of man.
"I don't care" is the attitude of those who have never needed a helping hand.

Some don't care because wealth provides a buffer against deficiency.
Others don't care because they wish to share their misery.

Some don't care because of the perception the world owes something.
Their lack of accumulation is the result of a stolen dream.

"I don't care" because they don't like me is based on a disturbed spirit.
The "I don't care" is an outward manifestation of self-pity.

The "I don't care" people try to paint a world of gloom.
The implication is given that we are all doomed.

In a competitive world the "I don't care" people feel the race has already ended.
To de-emphasize the victory, the vanquished display "I don't care to win it."

I Gave My Best

When it is over and done
When the task is complete and the war is won
Can you say, "I gave my best?"

Do you realize your reason for being?
Are you following or leading?

Life is measured in time and degrees.
You will disappoint and you will please.
But can you say--- I gave my best?

Is your best strong or is it weak?
Are you the best you can be?

Everything must be evaluated and done with a righteous heart.
Giving your best is a manifestation of your love for God.

God gave you the angles and the minutes.
Did He damage His world when He put you in it?
Can you truly say to your God, I gave my best?

Lie

In time, the fabricated character becomes the fact
The lie becomes big truth if not taken back.

Today's myth will become tomorrow's reality.
Give doubt a little time and it becomes a certainty.

Behind human falsehoods are diabolical plans.
Stretch and create character flaws to doom a man.

A man who stumbles will fall to a diabolical lie.
The fallen man is not beyond God's eye.

Perhaps the slave brought servitude upon himself.
Man has always been wicked and the future holds much more than death.

Character assassination needs justification to survive.
"See there" and "I told you so" is keeping the myths alive.

Tell the world the slave is a monster that must be chained.
Tell the slave, "God does not treat all men the same"

Telling the lie has always had evil intent.
The liar is hell bound if he does not repent.

Nail-Scared Hand

I was lost in a dark world with no life and void of light.
Hands reached for me but I would push them back.

I walked through this dark world and voices tried to pull me down.
I could not concentrate because the voices were all around.

Go here, Go there, Go back and Come here.
But this unknown world of sin brought me no fear.

I touched the hands because I am looking for the right one.
I walk in faith; therefore there was no cause to run.

A gentile hand almost deceived me because it was gentle to the touch.
I sought the light of the hand that can lift me from this rut.

Without my faith I would have been lost in darkness.
I knew I would find the light because I was and am blessed.

I would stumble along in this dark world looking for the right hand.
It was the knowledge of the truth that protects me from Satan.

One day I came to a cross-road in the dark but the Spirit showed me.
That day gave me a sense of purpose because the Spirit allows me to see.

And there in front of me was a hand extended in love.
I grab this nail-scared hand and it turned on a light from above.

Remember! People will extend a hand but you must reject them all.
Look for the nail-scared hand and you will be answering God's call.

Omni-Enemies

My enemies stand four abreast
But they will fall amass.

My enemies wait for helplessness
An opening will not come
My patience will last.

My enemies surround me with many traps.
They dehumanize my body and soil my name.
No peace brings no sleep but an occasional nap.
I suffer these indignities without blame.

Around the corner and over the hill, my enemies wait.
I will last and I will prevail.
God is my guide, therefore he controls my fate.
This precious soul was not made for Hell.

The Sin of the Kin

Each time the world looks into your eyes, a thousand lashes flash.
The world doesn't see you but the world sees all your kin of the past.

At first encounter the world already has an opinion of you.
The opinion is a mixture of facts, fiction and positive/negative too.

If your family history has an ounce of bad, you have much work in front of you.
A lie needs no facts to begin, to grow, to destroy or to prove it is true.

The true lie becomes the facts, if we want it to wound or kill.
The conscious is temporarily suppressed by blaming our actions on others' will.

No man is lie resistant nor can he make himself lie proof.
Christ was absolutely perfect but man lied on him too.

Each time the stranger looks at you, he seeks the worst of your kin.
You will have to account for both you and your family's sin.

An established reputation does not end with the death of the originator.
Misdeeds may lay low for ages but they always return sooner or later.

The Light of the World

When the night is black as it can be
There is always just enough light to see.

The light shineth all over the world all the time.
In a world full of dangers, in this light you will be fine.

There is comfort even in the darkest hour;
If you stay in this light's power.

There is power in a light that exposes everything
In this light all dangers can be seen

Follow this light, forever you will last.
It not easy to follow because it is off the desired path.

Though the path is not desired it is straight and pure.
With this light only the good can endure.

This darkness erasing light exposes all the way to the soul
A desperately needed light in a world that's dark and cold.

One must seek the light; it is there for everyone to see.
Look to the hill; the light weights, but you have to believe.

The Soothing Tears

A few blood-red tears will wash more than dirt from the eye.
It is a relief to the heart of man that is made to cry.

It is tears that ease the power of pain.
Tears can be hardly noticeable or flow like the rain.

Tears are a sign that something has changed.
The changes of life bring both joy and pain.

The tears of joy come from deep within.
The sad heart and the glad heart are influenced by sin.
Tears will be with us until sin is gone.
But there is no sin in God's heavenly home.

Tears soften the hard lines of age and time.
The teardrops follow the same downward line

Drop by drop falls until a puddle is formed.
The tears may stop long before the pain is gone.

The tears stop because reality is at hand.
The reality is man is evil and only God can change man.

The reality is we must forgive and move on.
All pain is temporal; therefore it will not stay for long.

Tears are good; they immediately wash away the hurt.
Tears wash the wound so pain does not sting so much.

Man's tears are bigger than the woman's tears.
Man seldom cries so his tears accumulate for years.

Women's eyes are bright and healthy because tears wash them regularly.
The child's first emotional response is to cry, so crying is an innate release.

People are the cause of most of the tears shed by man.
Relatively few tears are accidental, most are the result of a devious plan.

The Window

You have a window to your soul
I can see everything even warmth and cold.

You can't hide your soul because you got to see.
I am looking into you every time you look at me.

Your eyes flash a signal which I can read.
Your mouth can lie but your eyes can't deceive.

The lid tries to conceal but I understand the lash.
You try to hold it still but the lid's got to flash.

What is there in that soul you want to keep secret?
I can tell if it is a good or mean spirit.

The eye is the most important organ for finding out
about the world around you.

You use your eyes to gather knowledge,
I use your eyes to interview.

To show approval your pupils dilate.
The furrowed eyebrow and pupil can represent hate.

Those piercing eyes say don't mess with me.
The blue eyes can represent deceptive beauty.

The eyes can lead the heart to sin.
Close your eyes to temptation, you already know when.

"Whosoever looketh on a woman to lust after her hath
Committed adultery with her already in his heart" (Matt.5:28).

Your soul wants what it is seeing.
It is a natural feeling and pleasing.

The scripture told you your eyes can create mistakes.
The scripture solution - I don't think you can take.

"And if thy right eye offend thee, pluck it out,
And cast it from thee" (Matt.5:29.)

The eyes can create the feeling of ill will and discontent.
This is the Biblical evil eye of envy and resentment.

"Eat thou not the bread of him that hath an evil eye,
Neither desire thou his dainty meats" (Proverbs 23:6.)

Yes, I can look at your soul
I can tell if your heart is warm or cold.
There are many colors of the eye - black, brown, blue, green
And many shapes - round, oval, **doe**, slant and in-between.

From those eyes come direction from above:
Show approval, acceptance, friendship, give comfort
inspiration and love.

Let your heart come through your eyes in a good light.
Let us know you as a person of love and right.

A just person with a compassionate heart.
A person who lives the life and represents our God.

Two Fist Full of Dust

"And the Lord **GOD** formed man of the dust of the ground, and breathed into his nostrils the breath of life; and man became a living soul." Gen. 2:7
GOD had to process the soil to retrieve the dust.
It takes the finest particles to build a man of trust.

GOD knew that faithfulness could not be found in sand.
HE needed something **HE** could pack tightly to make a Holy man.

HE did not just want plain old soil.
Soil is full of matter that is easy to spoil.

HE could not use a rock; a rock takes an uncompromising stand.
Wet dust **HE** could mold into an obedient and righteous man.

Dirt represents a foul or filthy substance.
HE knew some dust would turn to dirt in some men and women.

GOD mixed this dust with water and whipped up a batch of clay.
HE was going to make beings that would honor Him in every way.

GOD did not have to toil all day.
To make this man it took only two fists of clay.

After making man, GOD put him in a beautiful place.
GOD saw he was a lonely creature with boring days.
GOD loved this being **HE** call man.
So **HE** took some of man's dust and made woman.

They were flesh of flesh, or one in two parts.
They were built in **GOD**'s image with pure hearts.

In time the devil tried to tear this down.
He promised man and woman an earthly crown.

I guess you could say he stirred up the dust.
GOD was left with men and women **HE** could not trust.

Sometime the devil injects a little sand.
This is how to create a sinful woman or man.

The devil injected soil and made them worldly.
Men and women became evil and un**holy**.

Sometime the wind blows the dust and scatters it around.
Wind can't move **holy** dust, it is firmly anchored down.

When it rains, some dust washes away.
Water doesn't erode **sanctified** dust, **GOD** made it to stay.

These two fists of dust can live for an eternity.
With their hand in **GOD**'s hand, they will always be free.

Wants and Needs

Everyone has wants and needs
Wants are not always deficient; they're also greed

Wants are desires, shortage and scarcities.
Needs are the more critical necessities.

What does a parent want from a child?
Wants are easy, can be as simple as a smile.

A parent wants a child to be safe and live.
A parent needs to receive the love a child can give.
A child needs the necessities the parent provides.
A child needs education and love to guarantee he will survive.

We all have to receive something from others.
This is why we use the terms sisters and brothers.

There is confusion in the kid we hold so dear.
They have yet to understand why we are here.

God expects us to live in an obedient way.
This means we have to control our impulses every day.

God wants us to Live

The children must learn. It is the parent's
God given duty to teach them the right way.
They must honor their parents, and show
Appreciation by doing what they say.

The Parent Needs the Child to Live

The parent cannot steer the child wrong.
The child knows wrong and should not go along.

This is a very evil time and all children are at risk.
The child must be patient, be aware and make rules persist.

A parent may seem overbearing and get in your way.
This is a parent's duty to guide and protect the child each day.

The child is naive and doesn't seem to know it.
Pleasure is primary and they show it.

To live as God intended does not come through.
They rebel against their parents and God too

The parent needs the child to live

Think about it! Why are we on this earth?
You have been on a mission since birth.

You are to go forth and multiply but in the right way
God's rule requires you remain obedient each day

We parents worry about you.
We want you to do right in everything you do.

We only have your best interest in mind.
We know maturity will take time.

So we guard you for as long as we can.
All young people are beautiful and can fall in devious hands.

The Godless are there waiting for the chance.
They will exploit you because you don't understand.

God, Freedom, & Trust

The young are too anxious to prove they are grown.
The unscrupulous will penetrate any unguarded home.

The parent needs the child to carry on their genes.
The child needs the parent to fulfill their dreams.

The child needs God for every achievement.
God needs the child to show love and always be obedient.

God wants the child to live.

It is not necessary that the child live.
God has many more souls to give.

The child wants the freedom to decide their fate.
Ignorant of this unforgiving world lack of sympathy for the mistake.

One mistake and they will need self-esteem.
Without that old confidence they cannot achieve their dream.
The parent needs the child to practice patience.
Don't make that first mistake, use common sense.

There is a very thin line between failure and the will to succeed.
The will is fragile and is lost on a few false needs.

Look out for love it is a tricky sort of wants and needs.
It is as intoxicating as liquor, cocaine, and weed.

The parent wants the child to always be in control.
The parent knows a little mistake can ruin souls.

Child! Show some maturity the parent needs it.
To turn an immature child out in the world the parent dies a little bit.

It up to the child to build confidence and show maturation.
They need to feel their child will be all right in any situation.

Child! You don't need to prove anything to anyone.
Watch every angle, protect your mind and still have fun.

God needs you morally to be the best you can be.
He is counting on the parent's guidance to help you see.

In this world there is far too much wrong.
Stick with your parent, you can't go it alone.

Where Is Peace?

On a hill overlooking a valley
I see no peace

In the valley and looking toward the hill
I see no peace

On a desolate country road
There is no peace

On a quiet lake and the fish biting
But there is no peace

When you bury the hatchet
You will uncover peace

Forget one's differences
Then you can remember peace

Smoke the pipe
Peace comes out of the smoke

In the grave
Peace is dead

Peace comes from contentment
And contentment comes from Heaven

The Birth of the Light

Early the first Christmas a light slowly emerged.

This is more than a change in heaven, this is the predicted birth.

From deep within a stable, a faint glow emerges from the hay.
Time slowed to a pulse, all motion stopped and sound went away.

Anticipation was so thick that you could pull it apart.
The unknown brings fear, so the motionless mind seeks God.

The faint flicker of light soon stops teasing the dark.
Now a definable glow is made available to all hearts.

The warmth of this glow was so divine that the animals turned in awe.
As the light in the stable emerged, so did the light of a heavenly star.

The glow in the hay was soon replaced by the sudden flash of a brilliant light.
The heavenly star flashes in syncopation as it signaled Good News to the night.

The stable now became the source of light much like the filaments of an incandescent bulb.
At 186,000 miles per second, this light moved toward every corner of the world.

The light moves through a dark world seeking the dark hearts of men.
The light is fast but its journey is made long by sin.

The light emerged from the holy night to expose the world to love.
The light will last for eternity because its power source is above.

Celebrate the light by directing it to your heart.
If you wish to live in the light, then removing sin is the start.

Salute

All over the world everything stopped.
There was no sound, total quietness.

The cricket did not chirp.
The baby did not burp.
The cock did not crow.
The wind did not blow.
The owl did not hoot.
All these actions were a salute

No sound, everything stopped.

The moon dimmed in salute.
All the stars, except one followed suit.
This one star lit the whole of the night.
One place on earth it showed very bright.

No limb from the tree broke.
Fire made no smoke
The waters became still.
Predators refuse to kill.

No sound, everything stopped.

The sleeping did not snore or grit their teeth.
All who were awake came to see.

But! They made no sound.

They stood in awe - “My god, what a star”

But! They made no sound.

In their mind something was happening that was great.
Fear set in, could this be the last day?
All at once the sleeping rose without a sound.
An unexpected force came to every town.
Without a sound they went outside.
The sight they saw opened all eyes wide.

But! They – made - no-- sound.

In their mind they knew this was a special day.
They all knew this was the Savior’s birthday
And the whole world kneeled down to pray.

The animals kneeled.
The fish came to the shore.
The birds bowed their head
And sin fell to the floor.

And yet! They – made - no - sound.

Later the world started moving again.
The Savior was visited by shepherds and wise men.
Now there are joyful sounds everywhere.
The once bright star is just a faded glare

When the sun rose, we saw a new earth.
Peace, Love, Hope, and Joy were brought by this birth.

The Thump and the UH

Thump, thump, thump is the sound
Uh, uh, uh is the sound

Eyes looked up and tears came down
Thump, uh, thump, uh can be heard around the world
Everywhere the overcast of sin was lifted by love

Thump, uh, thump, uh still can be heard
This is the day man tried to kill the word

The uh is not a Gods reaction to a physical torment
The only way to hurt a God is through disappointment

"My God why have thou forsaken me" is pointing directly at men
To hold back to walk away is to forsake and that is a sin

Look up at that cross and see the disappointment there
See my God who has done everything to show you he cares

But you refuse to return the love that was given so freely
As long as you know sin, my lord know no peace

From the thump and uh you should feel his pain
It takes yours and my salvation for his pain to end

Yes! He still feels the pains and he still carries the cross
He can't relinquish the burden until he save those who are lost

Stand up, carry the cross a little, and give the Lord a helping hand
Follow in his footstep and shine the light for your fellow man

Let the thump and the uh inspire you to carry the light
Attach you brothers to the vine before our savior comes back

The thump of the nail was a minor infliction
The agonizing pain came from the rejection

Pick up the cross and carry it for one who paid for you
This is a debt you owe, and it is way pass due

You Are Not My Brother

A true brother is more than one who shares a common ancestry, character, purpose or allegiance.
A true brother has a God loving heart that only eyes blind to this world can see.

My brother's Father is God and my brother is an heir to a distant throne.
My good-hearted brother will be with me for an eternity in our heavenly home.

My brother is more than a comrade, and closer than a friend.
He is a blood-washed kinsman from a chosen group called the brethren.

I am sometimes called brother by those with a common skin color.
The blood goes deeper than the skin and that does not make you my brother.

I am sometimes called brother because of a presumed common oppressor.
If you are not dependent on the Holy Spirit you are not my brother.

If greed is your driver, your life is about exploiting others.
You do not Love your neighbor, therefore you are not my brother.

You are selfish and place no value on the feelings of others.
You are capable of anything and you are not my brother.

Your secret lies with another's wife under darkness' cover.
You are lower than a snake and you are not my brother.

If you prey on the naivety of a gullible child, you are a deceiver.
You call yourself a player and counselor but you are not my brother.

If you take that which does not belong to you, you are a thieving sinner.
God knows your misdeed, you are not His child and you are not my brother.

If you disrespect the elderly, you dishonor your mother.
Your days are shortened, full of trouble and you are not my brother.

If you have no love, you will not know Joy and you will suffer.
Then Peace will not come because you are not my brother.

My spirit is longsuffering, gentle, good, faithful to my God and Kind to others.
If your life does not exhibit the Fruits of the Spirit you are not my brother.

If you like vulgar music and vulgar language, you are influencing the youngsters.
Then you are doing the work of the devil and you are not my brother.

If you beget a child out –of-wedlock, you are reproducing the fruit of two sinners.
You must beget offspring in a God ordained marriage if you are my brother.

If you hide in an intoxicated mind, you will not know your mother.
Drug induced euphoria will make wrong right, love hate and you are not my brother.

You have got to Believe!

Do you know that you could not get up in the morning
if you did not believe you could?

You cannot make a step if you don't believe you can.
If you want something done right give it to a believing man.

To walk a tightrope, your belief must be strong.
The courageous soldier in battle believes that he will make it home.

The victor in a gunfight believes in life.
The vanquished, less than perfect belief, gave him time to die.

The big dog believes in his invincibility because of his enormous size.
Even the big dog's belief dwindles when the pack arrives.

The small man is small only when he gives credence to the weakness of smallness.
The Christian is only a Christian when his belief is at its best.

The big man's confidence can be traced to the strength of his belief.
The wrong belief will bring death and much grief.

To believe is to have confidence in the truth.
If truth comes first, then how does truth come to you?

The truth is both heard and seen in true believers.
We hear the word and see "signs and wonders" (Act 5:12.)

We focus on our mission when we truly believe.
With the truth as our foundation there is nothing we cannot achieve.

The believer must be an example in word, conversation and charity. The world needs to see the believer's righteous spirit, his faith and his purity (1Tim. 4:12.)

The greatest of the believers' examples is the believer's LOVE or CHARITY (1Cor. 13:13.)

The Damned Parents

There is a thin imaginary line between good and bad.
But there is no acceptable boundary for the mom and dad.

In the child's eye the parent might be wrong or right.
To the child the parents' motivation is something they must fight.

The child can't see love because understanding comes with time.
How does one explain righteousness to an undeveloped mind?

Sensuous minds seek the pleasures of life without regard for cost.
Most of the parent's efforts are unappreciated and lost.

The parents don't seem to have the right to say no.
Children independently want to prove how much they know.

Children never consider that they are traveling an unfamiliar road.
The children secretly expect the parent to carry their load.

The parent is considered wrong to tell the ignorant child what is right.
The children impulsive desire for pleasure and position bring on the fight.

The ignorant child always confuses want with need.
The parent gives warning but the child refuses to heed.

So we are left with an imperfect cycle that perpetuates endless sin.
The chaos will probably go away if the children start listening.

They do not honor the damned parents because they aren't listening.
After the bumps and bruises they will find what they are missing.

But it will be too late to bring damnation to an end.
The children's children will start this cycle all over again.

The problems of society will never go away as long as children refuse to hear.
For every pain the damned parent feel the child will shed a tear.

The cycle of damnation is painful and it will go on until the child brings it to its end.
The longer the child's disobedience continues the greater becomes their sin.

In the future the child will try to shift the blame for their failure.
The parents are damned if they do and damned if they don't use the leather.

It is a no win situation, the child must do what other children do.
If one child sets a course for hell, he will take others too.

Vain

The empty words represent the empty hearts.
Man's life is vain because he has no time for God.

In a world of vanity can you believe anything written?
The motive is always suspected because the truth is hidden.

A man will call himself a Democrat or Republican because of one agenda item.
He blindly follows vain concepts that are designed to mislead him.

There is no substance there but he will never know it.
The misguided fool is caught up in chaos and he cannot quit.

It is all vanity and it cannot be right without righteousness.
We selfish humans should learn to care more not care less.

"I love you" means I love what you can do for me.
Lustful pleasure destroys the adult but the children never see.

The façade of this vain world does not expose the abuse our lives take.
The child never sees the truth until it makes the same mistake.

Unwedded mothers breed more unwedded mothers.
And the fathers of the bastard children call each other brother.

Brother is an empty word that is used as bait.
The word covers the eyes of the victim while the thief takes.

Sister is another empty word used primarily by the man.
Man use of sister has no gentile love because it is part of a devious plan.

A vain touch never really touches the sensitive skin.
Vain hugs miss the body and goes for the chin.

The Sunday school teacher makes a vain attempt in teaching the cross.
The ministers' vain attempt save not, but increases the number of loss.

Shallow words are spoken with the intention to deceive.
Vanity has left a world with nothing in which to believe.

Love now comes with strings attached.
It teases and pulls the victim to a place where he will never go back.

Empty love is a tool of deception that condemns the world.
It has moved from the adults, all the way down to pre-teen boys and girls.

Emptiness rides the periphery and cut down the middle of society.
Empty compassion and empty love has created a world of "No Mercy".
Empty purpose and empty opportunity will create "No motivation".
Apathy is an emptiness that will kill people and destroy a nation.

Empty words will devalue everything a body has to say.
Vain behavior desensitizes and turns emergencies into play.

When seriousness goes, vanity has sent it a way.
When chaos comes vanity causes it to stay.

Charity is driven by "what's in it for me".
Earthly rewards are the motivation for thank you and please.

Doing what is right in the eyes of God is the only way to eliminate vanity.
A true believer is full of the Holy Spirit; therefore his life is not empty.

Are profane words spoken by empty child of man with problems?
An ignorant child is ageless because vanity extends him.

15 years olds don't need a belt because the belt is below the buttocks.
He can never fall because his parents and drugs props him up.

12 year old girls are beauty queens that are allowed to go out on a date.
They look like half naked fashion models on the catwalk or a harlot on the make.

Vanity, it is all vanity

XIV The Land

This next section is about feeling close to the earth. Poems include the following:

1. **Reason for the Season**
2. **Sand**
3. **The City of New Orleans**
4. **The Lonely Oak**

Reason for the Seasons

Fall has its dog days
Spring's rain is out of place

Summer offers too much heat
Winter's cold brings ice, snow and sleet.

Seasons greet us and then say goodbye
Offer good and bad but no reason why

Why is there too much rain in one place?
And deserts have no water to waste

Why does summer heat go to extreme degrees?
And why must there be the winter freeze?

The wind also goes to the extreme when it blows.
The land is yearly bombarded with Hurricanes and Tornadoes.

Why does the season bring so much change?
Well, it is because it is part of God's plan.

Life is filled with the ups and the downs.
This is what makes the world go round.

There are plenty of bad and lots of good.
A world full of green trees got some dead wood.

God planned His world this way.
Remember! Your sins took some goodness away.

Every man has a task, and must carry his load.
Life is not easy, it is a rough road.

"Let us hear the conclusion of the whole matter: fear God, and keep His commandments: for this is the whole duty of man" (ECCLESIASTES 12:13.)

So don't worry about the effect of the seasons.
Everything is in God's hand and He has His reasons.

Sand

The waves of life roll toward the shore
Constant attacks the little grain must endure.

Helplessly caught in a cycle that never ends
Its existence is controlled by water and wind.

It is hard and brittle but then it must be
It is the buffer that separates land from sea.

It withstands wave after wave of attack.
The tide washes it out but the wind brings it back.

The wind molds it into giant dunes
But it is everywhere even on planets and moons.

Its' secret is that it knows how to give.
Without resistance it is allowed to live.

Sand has no will to stand and fight.
Wash and blow it away but it comes back.

Wave after wave can't wash it away
Gust after gust can't turn it to dust
Sand will be last because it was first.

The "City of New Orleans" Revisited 1954 - 2001

July 8, 2001, we ride the rails of Amtrak train.
Follow a route that has been traveled over and over again.

This path help settle the North much like the westward trails.
Hope for many migrating souls with only a body to sell.

The trail started in New Orleans but it sucked many souls from Mississippi
Many anxious and scared souls looking for America, the land of the free.

Many illiterate souls who could not read or write but had flesh and blood to give
Lost exploitable souls that believe the North will give them room to live.

It had to have been tough when whole families pulled up stakes and moved on.
Broken by the past but hopeful the family can be mended in a new home.

From the crowded cars they could see the life they were leaving outside the window.
Always dreading someone would burst into the train and take them back for more.

This is an escape route and even the boss man knows this is the way to freedom.
Many who ride this rail worry just like the escaped soul on the run.
Throughout the South everyone knew the names of the trains on these rails.
The "Panama Limit" and the "City of New Orleans" are the way out of hell.

They talk about these trains as if these trains were some great benevolent friends.
They had less fear of visiting the South because the Illinois Central trains could get them out again.

By far the "City of New Orleans" had the greatest fame.
The escape required speed and the "City of New Orleans" was the fastest train.

Yes! The "City of New Orleans" has brought hope to many that were hopeless.
It took them to the land of the free but true freedom will have to be blessed.

It was more than forty years ago when I rode the rail for the first time.
The cars are the only physical thing that has changed with time.

There are still a lot of Black people everywhere.
The most noticeable difference is the absence of fear.

From New Orleans to Chicago America looks like a Black land.
Inside and outside the train was the face of the Black man.

Maybe this is because the Black man has always lived over, under and across the track.
Even sitting in an overcrowded car for a long ride brought relief to the tired backs.

There were broken buildings and abandoned homes all along the rail.
The rail still passes through little towns and the backside of fields.

The train passes through farms that have not changed in over 40 years.
The timberland has changed, in many places it is totally cleared.

Forty years ago the "City of New Orleans" stopped in almost every town.
When the automobile came on the scene the train had to give ground.

Today's train is yesterdays express.
The trains stop at the major cities and pass up the rest.

The rail is old and in some areas the train sways a lot.
Forty years later old Black men still gather at the same spot.

The tracks have always been the border between the "haves" and the "have-nots."
"Across the tracks" shirtless Black boys play street ball in a vacant lot.

The train rumbles and sways as it passes through the marsh and wetland.
The swampy area is the home of Charlie the alligator and quicksand.

Jackson, Mississippi, was the first major city on the escape route to the North.
This was a hub city that injected lost souls from the East and West.

The Jackson station was a large terminal, designed to accommodate many travelers.
This was usually not the destination; it was mainly a place to transfer.

Throughout North Mississippi the route included many little Box Lunch stops with depots.
From these little towns the warm bodies continue to flow.

From Tennessee, Kentucky, and Arkansas the suction continued to remove man.
The tracks crossed into Illinois, a place of large cornfields and the promise land.

The trip through Illinois seems to have taken days.
There was flat farmland almost all the way.

Then the little towns appeared one right after the other.
Soon the town came so frequent that they seemed to be connected together.

The commuter trains running parallel to the "City of New Orleans" indicate the suburbs.
Anticipation increases because we were not far from the little station on 63rd.

Joy is almost at its maximum when the conductor calls out 63rd street station.
This was almost the end of the line for a major route for mass migration.

This is Chicago the city of the free!
It opened its doors to many temporary laborers who refused to leave.

The "South Side" and the "West Side" are where the farm hand found his cousin.
They were refugees from De Facto slavery who felt like condemned men.

The "City of New Orleans" took them to Chicago downtown.
They dispersed to comfortable locations and others moved on to higher ground.

Through the Chicago station they moved to the surrounding states.
The "City of New Orleans" added color to the Midwest and it never was late.

The Lonely Oak

I could see this big oak tree looking at me.
In my mind I could hear, "save me"

I knew it couldn't be this tree.

It was though a spell was cast over me.
Because I still heard the words, "save me"

I looked around at all that I could see,
But it seemed this big oak was looking at me.

I focused my eyes and my heart on this tree,
Because I needed to know if it was calling out to me.

I took my steps in groups of three,
Because I must get closer to this tree

Up close the sun I could not see
This is when I realized the massiveness of this tree.

Everywhere there were pines around this oak tree.
Now I understand why it calls out to me.

This big oak is hurting it seems to me,
because it's whole family is deceased.

Everywhere man has destroyed the oak tree.
Man has replaced the oak with the money tree.

There were no other oaks to see.
This is a lonely and hurting tree.

I touched it on its trunk and its leaf,
to reassure it, it has a friend in me.

I went to other lands and found acorns on the ground.
I brought them back and spread them all around.

The big oak bowed to me.
I knew it appreciated the seeds.

Two years later I went back to visit this tree.
Little oak trees were all around me.

I looked at the big oak tree.
It showed joy and thankfulness to me.

This reaction felt real good to me.
I will forever listen to a tree.

XV Song Lyrics

This section contains songs that floated out of the air after a prodding from the moment. The songs include the following:

1. **Dis Ole Lady**
2. **Go On Home**
3. **He Is my Friend and God**
4. **I Am Ready**
5. **I Am Ready to Go Home**
6. **I Cannot Let It Go**
7. **I Know Sin Follows Me**
8. **I Walk the Waters of Freedom**
9. **In a Cold, Cold World**
10. **I've Been Walking with My Jesus**
11. **Not Alone**
12. **Oh! Dying Soul**
13. **There Has Got to Be More**
14. **This Is the Morning**
15. **When Our Day Is Nigh**
16. **When We Are Down**
17. **I Remember**
18. **Joy Is Here**
19. **You Can't Get to Heaven on Your Own**
20. **I Don't Understand**
21. **I Was Lost**

22. There Has Got to Be More
23. Why We Live
24. I Will Do Something Good for Me
25. Amazing Grace the Inner Peace
26. She Is Just a Baby
27. What about Us
28. What Did I Say
29. Heavenly Father

Dis Ole Lady

1.
Dis Ole lady ain't what she used to be
Dis Ole lady ain't what she used to be
Dis Ole lady ain't what she used to be

But she still our Mom
Lord!! She still our Mom

2.
Dis Ole lady still our mom
Dis Ole lady still our mom
Dis Ole lady still our mom

But she'll go on and on
Lord!!! She must go on

3.
Dis Ole lady birthed seven children
Dis Ole lady birthed seven children
Dis Ole lady birthed seven children

She done real fine
Because God was her best friend.

4.
Dis Ole lady had to work real hard
Dis Ole lady had to work real hard
Dis Ole lady had to work real hard

Lord!!! She came through
By the power of God

5.
Dis Ole lady cried many tears
Dis Ole lady cried many tears
Dis Ole lady cried many tears

Lord!!! With her faith
She has no fears

6.
Dis Ole lady has known poverty.
Dis Ole lady has known poverty.
Dis Ole lady has known poverty.

Lord!!! She is rich
Because her spirit is free

7.
Dis Ole lady has earned her celebration.
Dis Ole lady has earned her celebration
Dis Ole lady has earned her celebration

Lord!!! A mother's love
Has blessed her daughters and sons

Go on Home

Go on home; Go on home, I'll see you again someday
Go on home; Go on home, I'll see you again someday

I'll be here---------but wait there for me-----
I'll be there someday-----
I'll be there ------ I'll be there ------I'll be with you--- again---------

My Father's house, -- My Father's house is where we will meet again----
You go there, you go there--------, but will you wait for me----------
Will you wait for me? Will you wait for me?

Death is just a doorway to my Father's kingdom.
It is a time to say farewell to another saint who is moving on.

Life is so temporary and can be thought of as a test.
To move to my Father's house you must be at your best.

The only way to live forever is to shed mortality.
All our life work should be directed toward this dreaded reality.

Death may bring cessation of human consciousness but it also brings hope of resurrection.
"…. It is appointed unto men once to die"; which means God sets the time of our transition.

The last enemy is destroyed now because death is dead for the deceased.
A Christian knows that "absence from the body" will bring ultimate peace.

There is no need to cry, no need to dread and no need to fear.
If the soul has been regenerated then our Lord will be there.

But if the soul goes only to a place of silence there is nothing you can do.
Repentance is dead for the deceased but your transition is up to you.

It is alright to cry for the dead and the love that might have been.
But also shed some tears for a world deep in the grip of sin.

It is alright to wail, mourn, wear sackcloth, put ashes on your head, and tear your clothes.
Your lamentation comes from a spiritual essence that only you and God know.

So cry my friend, cry for those who has gone on
But save some of your tears for the living who walk alone and mourn.

Our earthly life will cease and there is no way to avoid physical death.
The living must seek my Father's house because only dread is left.

We don't have to say goodbye, just say I will see you later.
But don't forget to say I am glad you've gone to something better

Just say wait on the other side till I come
I am too busy working for my Father but soon my work will be done

Go on home; Go on home, I'll be with you someday
Go on home; Go on home, I'll be with you someday

I'll be with you someday
My Father's house got many mansions; I'll be there some day
I'll be there, I'll be there I'll be there real soon
Sleep for now, rest a while I'll be with you real soon

Jesus waits, Jesus waits, waits for you and me
Waits for you and me Waits for you and me

He Is My Friend and God

My Lord so loved me that he gave His only begotten Son to free me.
The Lord is my light when the world is too dark to see.
I am but a poor sinful soul -------------------------and my Lord still loves me.

Because He ----- is my----- Friend --------------- and God----------

Yea, though I walk through death's valley, fear does not stand
The Lord who conquered death is holding my hand.
He --knows our troubles -------------------------------because He has walked with man 'cause He ----- is my ------Friend --------------- and God---------

It is God that girdeth me with strength and maketh my way perfect best
Thou wilt shew me the path of life in thy presence is fullness of joy
This is all I ask please --------------------------------guide me through the test

He ----- is my------- Friend --------------- and God------------

The Lord is my rock and my fortress and deliverer
My God is my strength, in whom I will trust
This is more than I deserve---------------------------------- please God save

He ----- is my--------- Friend --------------- and God----------

The Lord is my buckler and the horn of my salvation and my high tower
I will fear no evil because I am within His power.
This is all I ask, He is God

He ----- is my--------- Friend ---------------- and God----------

Thou has given me shield of my salvation: and thy right hath holden me up and thy Lord
This is all that I ask from my God, Please God
Oh--------------Lord---------------------
Where can I go but to you?

I am ready to go with You anytime.
Lord, take!

He has done more than I deserve
To be with Him is all that I ask from my God

He ----- is my -----------Friend ---------------- and God-----------

Thou has given me shield of my salvation: and thy right hath holden me up, and Thy gentleness hath made me great
He ----- is my Friend ---------------- and God
This is my request please God!!!

I can't take anymore. I want to come home

I Am Ready

When sin is so deep, it seems there is no way out.
Just remember peace is what the second coming is all about

Because He'll come back, and will you be ready my friend.
To walk with my God and live with Him (for a 1000 years)?

So take my hand, for I walk with God; I am ready.

I am ready for the Kingdom to come; Oh, Lord.
(Yes, I am ready.)
There will be no more mornings to come
There will be no more evening suns
And the night will never come

And I am ready
For the Kingdom to come.

Because He'll come back; and will you be ready
To walk with my God and live with Him for a 1000 years?

There will be no more tears and sorrow.
There will be no need for hope for tomorrow.

Cause He'll come back, and I will be ready to live with my God for a 1000 years. (Oh, Lord!)

This will be just the beginning of eternity
I am ready because New Jerusalem waits for me.

I am ready for the kingdom to come, oh, Lord!
(Yes, I am ready!)

There will be no more mornings to come.
There will be no more evening suns.
And the night will never come.

And I am ready for the Kingdom to come

I Am Ready to Go Home My Friend

The rain comes down---- it brings so much pain – my friend

The time has come -------to take ----my final bow---------

The world is cold ----- and I – have-- no more warmth – to give – my friend

I am ready ---------- to go home -----

I sing my last song ----- the gate has begun--- to close for me my friend

There are no more curtains – in front--- of-me-----

My bags are packed – my traveling---- shoes—are all a glow my friend

I am ready ---- to- go- home

Shed no tears ------ no tears for me – I know I----- must leave
Leave ---- a cold---world ---behind me---
The world—has—turned black ----- and it's getting dark outside----
It time-------to close the door------ my friend

I am ready ------to go home
My pain is behind me now

I still ----- feel --- strong ------- though life ---- leaves me slow and in the rain.
My hands are warm----- when yours are so --- cold my friend.
I am ready to go home

(The road has ended ----- I got no place to go ---- my friend)

I am ready ---- to take --- my final bow

I have given all ------I-- had to give------
Given all --- that I own----
Time has come --- and there are no more tomorrows

I am ready – to go home now
So close the door---- so I can leave the cold behind
I am ready to go home

I cannot let it go

I cannot let it go.
It pains me far too hard.

I must let it go,
Because I've given it to God.

I cannot let it go.
The wound is so deep it still bleeds.
I can only find relief when I am on my knees.

I tried to forgive, but I simply cannot forget.
How can I forget when my brother doesn't repent?

The battle may have subsided, but my enemies have no end.
But I will keep on trying to forgive the deeds of men.

But I cannot let it go.
I'm too hurt to forget.

I'm no longer drowning, but I am still wet.

I cannot let it go.
It pains me far too hard.

I must let it go,
Because I've given it to God.

I have to let it go, even if my brother doesn't repent
I know I can bear the pain because my tolerance is heaven sent.

They've knock me down, beat me up and slapped me all around
But there is no way they can break me and tear my faith in God down.

No!   No!   No!
I cannot let it go.
But I will forgive the pain as long as I live.

I cannot let it go.
It pains me far too hard.

I must let it go,
Because I've given it to God.

I Know Sin Follows Me at a Distance because I Am Going Home

I know sin follows me at a distance because I am going home.
I know sin follows me at a distance because I am going home.

I don't worry because of the road I trod, I am on my way home.
My home is up there with my God, I am going home.

I know where this rough road leads. I am going home-----------
I follow the bloody footprint in front of me. I am going home---------
I know sin follows me at a distance because I am going home.
I know sin follows me at a distance because I am going home.

I don't know about tomorrow, because I am going home.
My road is called sorrow but I am going home.
I follow the way my Jesus walked, I am going Home---
I talk the way my Jesus talked, to find my way home.
I know sin follows me at a distance because I am going home.
I know sin follows me at a distance because I am going home.

My road gets rough and my road get hard, I am going home—
I know home is with my God
I know sin follows me at a distance because I am going home.
I know sin follows me at a distance because I am going home.
I know sin follows me at a distance because I am going home.

I Walk the Waters of Freedom

I walk the waters of freedom, it cannot be too deep.
I walk the waters of freedom and Jesus waits for me.

My faith in Jesus is whole and I'll get to the other side.
My life has been perfected by the trial and the tears I cry.

I walk the waters of freedom, and Jesus urges me on.
He said, "You must follow me, if you want to get home."

I walk the waters of freedom, it cannot be too deep.
I walk the waters of freedom and Jesus waits for me.

My eyes are on Jesus; my faith is complete.
He guides my soul with His Spirit to eternity.

He took my heart in His hand and molded it to His name.
I stop treading water and my life will never be the same.

I walk the waters of freedom, it cannot be too deep.
I walk the waters of freedom and Jesus waits for me.

When He came into my life I began to see the other bank.
As long as my eyes remain on Jesus, I don't have time to sink.

One day I will touch His wonderful hand, and then I'll know I made it across.
If it wasn't for the cross I would surely have been among the lost.

I walk the waters of freedom, it cannot be too deep.
I walk the waters of freedom and Jesus waits for me.

In a Cold, Cold World

Life is filled with pain and each day will come again but Jesus will watch over me
I cannot find release but I live in peace because Jesus stands with me

In a cold, cold world it touches me so deep to know that somebody did something for me.

I found hope in His word and salvation in His blood because Jesus died for me
I will not die alone; I have someone to depend on because Jesus, He carries me.

In a cold, cold world it touches me so deep to know that somebody did something for me.
In a cold, cold world it touches me so deep to know that somebody did something for me.

When He died upon the cross all my sins were loss because Jesus paid the cost for me.
For me He had to die; now I can't help but cry, because Jesus was the Lamb for me.

In a cold, cold world it touches me so deep to know that somebody did something for me.
In a cold, cold world it touches me so deep to know that somebody did something for me.

I've Been Walking with My Jesus

Verse #1
I've been walking with my Jesus
I've been walking with my God
He took my hand and led me to the bright light.
Now everything is clear to me
(Now salvation is within reach)

Verse #2
I've been walking with my Jesus
I've been walking with my God
He has showed me a place of many mansions.
And I will be going there with him.

Verse #3
I've been walking with my Jesus
I've been walking with my God
I got my eyes on the prize and I know
I will never turn ------ back
(This redeemed soul will never turn back)

Verse #4
I've been walking with my Jesus
I've been walking with my God
His love for me is so superior ----Oh Lord
He has brought salvation to me.

Verse #5
I've been walking with my Jesus
I've been walking with my God
One day he'll come in the clouds above me.
And then He will take me right on back.

Verse #6
If you will walk with my Jesus
You will be walking with my God
They are one and same with the Spirit
That is why we call them Lord

Verse #7
You must walk with my Jesus
If you want to walk with God
You will walk your way to heaven
In the footsteps of the Son of Man

Not Alone

Not alone as I walk this sad land alone.
I passed yesterday tomorrow on my own

There is no flesh and blood that can please me because I am not alone.
I pass never as I travel in search of home, but not alone.

I have someone who holds my hand, as I travel among men, but not alone.
I climb the bloody hills and death valleys, it seems alone,
but I am not alone.

The slave I see but he does not smile back at me, but he is not alone.
The lady offers more than a hand to me alone, but I am not alone.

The children neither smile nor cry for they are not alone.
Not alone as I walk the dusty water of the city, yes! Not alone.

I pass groups of soul shells that blow in the wind all alone.
The preacher man with no bible stands in the crowd but he is alone.

But I am not alone

Not alone because my hand holds fast to His hand, and He carries me
for a distance. I cannot see.
Not alone!

The sea engulfs the land, and sings a sad song they cannot hear; they
are alone.

He carried the burden as He stumbled alone, but He is not alone.
Therefore, I am not alone.

Each step left a trail of tear-scared blood through the wounded street as He is not alone!

He and the thorns are raised in loneliness.

Not alone as He has to guide me through life's test.

He lay down on the timbered ground to give for me, so I can't be alone.

I close my eyes for I cannot bear what I see, but I am not alone.

They raise the flag of love and salvation but I am not alone.

My tears hit the ground and merge with His blood and flow.
Not alone!

He held my eye until His blood was gone but my tears remained.
Not alone!

To the cold room they carried Him into the dark, but He was not alone.

He shall rise; He said He would within three days.

Within three days the dark will cease and death will die.
Not alone!

I saw the one as I walked the dusty road to Emmaus, not alone!

I am not alone though the clouds cover Him completely.
Not alone!

Oh! Dying Soul

Oh! Dying soul, the Lord, the Lord is calling.
His solicitous voice appeals far and wide.
He sent His Son to die for the dying,
But you deny and push Him aside.

But He'll be back when clouds make no shadow
And when the trump begins to blow.
The dead will meet Him without a shadow
And at this time, at this time you will want to go.

And when He comes, don't be caught napping
For no man knows the day or the hour that shall be.
If you are not chosen, it is too late for crying
But you can still pray for "mercy please."

He may hear though millions converse above thee
That your hope of strong delusions shall not be.
The end is not here and tribulations shall not flee,
But even in this darkest hour there is hope for thee.

Oh! Dying soul, the Lord, the Lord is calling.
His solicitous voice appeals far and wide.
He sent His Son to die for the dying,
But you deny and push Him aside.

There Has Got to Be More

This can't be all to this life; there has got to be more.

There has got to be more.
In a world full of sin, there has got to be a door.
There has got to be more.

I looked up at the sky, and I don't understand the wonder of it all.
There is much more to this world that prevents the fall.
There has got to be more.

There has got to be something or someone that watches over us.
My life is in the hand of someone I can trust.

This can't be all to this life; there's got to be much more.
To every moment there is a why.

This can't be all to this life; there is got to be much more.
There has got to be more.
Every moment has an end time, but where is the door.

My God looks out for me in my every living moment, He is there for me.
A loving Creator built this world and everything in it.

This can't be all to this life I live.
I receive freely what the Creator has to give.

This can't be all because we need so much more.
I will always love my God and his blessing until it is time to go.

This can't be all to this life; there is so much more.

And when it is time, I will go peacefully to my heavenly room.
There is more to this life, and we will all know real soon.
There has got to be more.
Sometime I don't understand; but my faith is strong, and my life is in His hand.
Someday! With help from above I will take flight with the wing of a dove.
Then I will know how much more.

Cause there has got to be more!

The Morning

This is the morning. This is the morning.
This is the end of my life-long torment and fight with evil.
The Lord will meet me.
The Lord will meet me in the morning.

I can no longer go through an empty life
The Lord waits for me at the final river; I shall go across to meet Him.
He'll take my hand.
He is my Friend and God!
My Lord! Oh, my Lord!
I love to go with You in the morning.
I am ready this morning; please, God, take me.

This is the morning.
My Lord waits on the other side.
He waves to me to come to Him to live in everlasting peace.

My Lord waits beyond the river.
My heart aches because I've seen Him.
This world will die.

This is my departure because I've stayed too long.
Too long to live!

When Our Day Is Nigh

When our day is nigh,
We shall never see the change.

When our day is nigh,
Men shall call his name in vain.

(Repeat both verses)

Brother shall betray brother even unto death.
Brother will take brother's body to himself.

When our day is nigh,
We shall bring great pain.

Father forsakes the family and betrays the son.
Sin birthed the battle the moment the child was born.

When our day is nigh,
We shall never see the change.

When our day is nigh,
We shall forget his name.

Children shall rise up against their parents and live without care.
Godless children will put their womb to death.

The saints shall be hated for the way they live,
But they shall endure because of the love that they give.

When our day is nigh,
We shall never see the change.

When our day is nigh,
Men shall call his name in vain.

Man hath put asunder what God has jointed into one.
Man now breaks all the rules and eternal life is gone.

(Repeat chorus)

When We Are Down

When one of us is down,
We must all come around
And lend a helping hand
To do all that we can to help him stand.
Remember! When pain comes to one
Our work has just begun.
We cannot stop till our work is fully done
Where pain has ceased and is on the run.

When one of us is down,
We must all come around
And lend a helping hand
To do all that we can to help him stand.

Remember! When Christ came to the earth
He came through a miraculous birth.
We must always put His commandments first
Only Christ like love can heal the hurt.

When one of us is down,
We must all come around
And lend a helping hand
To do all that we can to help him stand.

Always remember! We can conquer if we pray.
Christ will timely take all our discomforts away.
Our hands of support will always stay.
Hand-in-hand we will move along the way.

When one of us is down,
We must all come around
And lend a helping hand
To do all that we can to help him stand.
Remember! God will prevent the fall
If you give Him your all-and-all.
We are here because of God's call.
With faith in God there are no walls.

When one of us is down,
We must all come around
And lend a helping hand
To do all that we can to help him stand.

When one of us is down,
It is time for the rest to gather around
To find victory in despair
To show the dying world that we care.

When one of us is down,
We must all come around
And lend a helping hand
To do all that we can to help him stand.

Pain may come and never seem to go.
Find comfort in knowing God loves you so;
But when one of us is down,
It is His love that gathers around.

When one of us is down,
We must all come around
And lend a helping hand
To do all that we can to help him stand.

I Remember

The sun shall rise and the moon follows later on.
Each day is a cycle of life, but I won't be alone.

I remember when the world was such a sweet place to be.
I remember Mom and the warmth of her arms.

I remember, my friends! How my parents took good care of me.
And I remember the love that they showed.
When I was young and when I was old
I was warm when it was cold.
It was a village of love that kept me warm.

I remember the home-cooked meals we shared at home.
I remember the prayer my father prayed when he was alone.
I remember the games we played
And all the hot and cold days. I remember it well; it is still inside of me.

I remember Father reading his Bible by the fire light.
I remember his face with the tear track.

He was strong enough to carry his family on his back.
Oh! Yes, I remember it well! Oh! Yes, I remember it well

Some days my mind takes me back home.
I travel the dusty road my grandpa traveled on.
Oh, yea, I remember it all. I have total recall.
My mind sees it; my mind thinks it; there is no future because it is inside of me.

Because I remember when the world was such a sweet place to be.
I remember Mom and the warmth of her arms.

I saw Grandma and sweet potato pie on the stove.
Oh! Yes, I remember it well! Oh! Yes, I remember it well
Oh! Yes, I remember it well

I saw brother carrying the firewood load. Oh! Yea, such a heavy load!
Oh! Yea, such a heavy load!
I open my eyes to see the old rustic house in front of me
And a smiling family stood waiting on me,
Oh! Yes, waiting on me! Oh, yes they were waiting on me.

Because I remember when the world was such a sweet place to be.
I remember mom and the warmth of her arms.

Joy is Here, NLCO Version

Joy is here,
Joy is here,
Joy is here today.

I know I been Redeemed.
My sins left behind.
Joy is here to stay

Verse:
When I was born,
I did not understand,
But the Lord brought me through.

I learned to go to my knees,
My sins started to flee
Now I know Love is here to stay.

Love is here
Love is here,
Love is here today.

I know I been Redeemed.
My sins left behind.
Love is here to stay

Verse:
When I started my day
Satan came to play
I knew the Lord would make a way

I looked straight above
I saw His glorious love
Then I started dancing the dance of Happiness

Happiness is here,
Happiness is here,
Happiness is here today.

I know I been Redeemed.
My sins left behind.
Happiness is here to stay

Verse:
When the sun went down
Trouble was still around
But Holy is the ground

I bowed my head in prayer
The Lord was still there
I went to bed resting in peace

Peace is here,
Peace is here,
Peace is here today.

I know I been Redeemed.
My sins left behind.
Peace is here to stay

Verse:
I tossed and turn through the night
Satan rode my back.
But my bible put him to flight.

I showed him John 3:16.
Then he left my dream.
I followed the love of Jesus to Liberty.

Liberty is here,
Liberty is here,
Liberty is here today.

I know I been Redeemed.
My sins left behind.
Liberty is here to stay

Verse:
The world was pulling me down.
I once was chained and bounded.
But Jesus placed my feet on solid ground.

I confessed my shackles to Him.
He gave me the keys to them.
I walked away shouting my victory

Victory is here,
Victory is here,
Victory is here today.

I know I been Redeemed.
My sins left behind.
Victory is here to stay

Verse:
Now I know where I'm going.
Cause I've been reborn
Thanks! To the wonderful Son.

Peace is not a dream
I know I've been redeem
I got to tell you about my Freedom.

Freedom is here,
Freedom is here,
Freedom is here today.

I know I been Redeemed.
My sins left behind.
Freedom is here to stay

Can continue with these verses below.

- Kingdom is here
- Heaven is here
- Christ is here
- Life is here

You Can't Get to Heaven on Your Own

You know, you can't get to heaven on your own.
You can't get to heaven on your own.

You can try with all your might.
You may move ahead but you will fall back.

Cause, you can't get –to heaven on your own.

You can't get to heaven on your own. (on your own.)
You **can't get to heaven on your own**

You must take others with you
As you travel up the milky white way.

Cause, you can't travel this way alone--.

No, you can't get to heaven on your own.
No, **you can't get to heaven on your own.**

When you reach for the hand of Jesus,
You must seek other hands to trust.

Cause, you need a helping hand to get home.

You Can't Get to Heaven on your own.
You can't get to heaven on your own.

Two steps forward and three steps back.
The world will pull you of your track.

Cause you will sink in the miry clay on your own.

You know you can't get to heaven on your own.
You know you can't get to heaven on your own!

You will meet many smiling faces.
They will pull you to other places.

Cause you can't fight temptation on your own.

You can't get to heaven on your own.
You can't get to heaven on your own!

You may fall on your knees and ask the Lord for Heaven above
But my Lord is telling you, to share His Love
Cause you got to love somebody to get home.

I Don't Understand

Sometimes I get lost and confused.
Sometimes I will seek peace through God's rules.

How can I go through life's long journey?
How can I remain true?

I go on seeking hand after hand.
I pray God I help save a damned man.

Why! Why! I don't understand.
I pray God to forgive and take my hand.

I know now that love is the key.
I thank God for putting so much love on me.

I know love is the key.
I can't do right for God if I don't do right by you.

We go through life, but we don't understand.

One day we will understand.
But in the meantime, we must seek His hand.

I know He is there; my heart tells me true.
I can't do right by my God if I can't do right by you.

My knees are weak; I fall to the ground.
I reach for God's hand, but man pulls me back down.

I beg God to have mercy, please.
Touch my heart and make me sin free.

Time moves on it, waits for no one.
One day our place will be gone, but our hearts will live on.

My God, I don't understand.
Why is love so very hard for man?

I fall down; I fall to my knees
I beg, God, have mercy please; touch my heart and make me sin free.

My! Oh my, I can't understand.
I pray to God for your health and that you fully understand that we must all understand.

We can go on forever, but we need love to grow.
We need God's gentle hand to help us understand.

Look to tomorrow and count your blessings.
God's love is real, and it will never lessen.

We can see God in everything we see.
We must show God in everything we do.

Days will flow but each moment is time.
There is no end, but there is a line.

We can't get there if we don't understand.
You can't do right by God if you hate man.

You can't do right by God if you can't do right by me.
I look at you, and God is what I hope to see.

We have no goals if we don't understand.
What is pleasing to God is love among man.

We will have sorrow and experience great pain.
The cure starts when we try to understand.

If you don't understand, you will hate time.
Your pain will come when you cross the line.
A pain without end awaits the blind.
Your future is no gamble, if you understand.

Try as I might but I cannot understand why there is so much hurt in a world that's going to end, (soon will end).

I know God will pull me through because He looks after me, and He will look after you.

Life goes on, but we don't understand.

How can I feel this way? I gave love to this world and the world threw it away.

I've done wrong, but I didn't understand.
I pray God will forgive all man.

Time goes on beyond the ending.
Where shall I go at the end?

Time goes on, and where I know not.
Jesus is with me and He is all I got.
Time is gone, and I've lost everything I had.
Now my hope is at its end, and I feel so sad.

Time goes, and I can't understand.
I pray God will keep me true to the end.

I Was Lost

I was lost in a world full of deadly sin
Couldn't find my way out though I tried over and over again.
I was lost in the dark and alone.
I cannot find my way back to my sacred home.

I was lost on my own.
Where is salvation? Where is hope?
I've climbed the highest mountain and descended the steepest slope,
But I can't find my way.
It is so dark; I cannot tell night from day.
Sometimes it seem as though it is all over

I was lost.
I was lost in a world full of sin.
Every time I rise, I am knocked down again.
I need rest but no sleep cometh. I am too lost to sin.
I was following the dead-end and found a place I had already been.

I was lost.
I've look beneath the rock for what escapes me.
I've searched for the helping hand, but it is too dark to see.
There is no light, but there is still hope.

I have stumbled and found myself on a slippery slope.
My ladder's too short and my rope is broke.
Sometimes it seems it is all over.
Where can I look? What will I find? What will I feel?
I am so confused I do not know if I am for real.
I stretch my arm to God and pray for His grace.

I was lost.
I was lost in a world full of sin.
Every time I get a glimpse of God, my view is blocked by selfish men.

I climbed to the mountaintop only to fall down again.
I keep searching, but I don't know where or when.
I was lost in a world full of deadly sin
Couldn't find my way out though I tried over and over again.
I was lost in the dark and alone.
I cannot find my way back to my sacred home.

There Has Got to Be More

This can't be all to this life, there has got to be more.

There has got to be more.
In a world full of sin, there has got to be a door.
There has got to be more.

I looked up at the sky, and I don't understand the wonder of it all.
There is much more to this world that prevents the fall.
There has got to be more.

There's got to be something or someone that watches over us.
My life is in the hand of someone I can trust.

This can't be all to this life; there's got to be much more.
To every moment there is a why.

This can't be all to this life; there's got to be much more.
There has got to be more.
Every moment has an end time, but where is the door.

My God looks out for me in my every living moment, He is there for me.
A loving creator built this world and everything in it.

This can't be all to this life I live.
I receive freely what the Creator had to give.

This can't be all because we need so much more.
I will always love my God and his blessing until it is time to go.

This can't be all to this life there is so much more.

And when it is time, I will go peacefully to my heavenly room.
There is more to this life, and we will all know real soon.
There has got to be more.
Sometime I don't understand; but my faith is strong, and my life is in His hand.
(Someday, with help from above, I will take flight with the wings of a dove.)
Cause! There has got to be more.
(Then I will know how much more.)

Why We Live?

Why do we live? Oh! Why- do we live?
If not to serve our Master, then why do we live?

Why do we live? Oh! Why do we live?
If not to serve our Savior, then tell me why do we live?

Our lives should be His life. Our care should be His care.
Our love should be His love, to show that Jesus is here
Oh! Why do we live? Oh! Why do we live?
If not to serve my Jesus, then why do we live?

We are to do the work of the Lord; He left us a task to do.
If you believe in my Jesus, His work you will gladly do.

Then, why believe? Then, why believe?
If you don't want to be with Jesus, then why believe?

Why should we change?
Why should we believe?
He made salvation possible Exposing eternity.

For all have sinned. For all have sinned.
You can change and believe Him,
For all have sinned.

Then why do we believe?
Why do we believe?
It is the only way to heaven and eternal peace.

I Will Do Something Good For Me

This morning was like no other morning, with the sun came realization too.
My future lies in front of me, so what am I going to do.

I can't reach back and change the past, but I can control something I have yet to see.
I will seek the future on God's terms and do something good for me.

I will seek the future on God's terms and do something good for me.
I got out of bed and looked around to see what do I truly own.
Reality says, I only had time that was mine and now most of it is gone.

I finally realized that there is no material thing that belongs to me.
So I will seek the future on God's terms and do something good for me.

I sat there on the side of my bed and asked myself, "Are you ready for today?
Shall this day's journey be smooth sailing or will it's time just drift away?"

It, just now, occurred to me that all of life's decisions are very easy.
All I have to do is seek the future on God's terms and do something good for me.

As I made my way to the bathroom, my whole spirit seemed to rise.
I no longer dreaded my dead-end job; in fact, I was anxious to go outside.

I feel good about myself, and I'd like to open the world's eyes to what I see.
All they have to do is seek the future on God's terms and feel good just like me.

All I have to do is seek the future on God's terms and do something good for me.

I thought as I set out to earn my pay everything I own will be lost if today is my last day.

If you go into the future outside God's terms, it will cause much anxiety, lost time and maybe some pain.
Continuous ups and downs will complete a cycle and start all over like sunshine and rain.

Losses may include my luxury car and the big house on the hill.
Man exists on a hope and a prayer because he does not know God's will.

There is one thing I know that others cannot see.
I will seek the future on God's terms and do something good for me.

I will seek the future on God's terms and do something good for me.

I think about the spouse and just how long will we be together.
Are we on the same path to keep us together in the hereafter?

And there are the children; they will be included in the permanency of eternity.
I must show them how to seek the future on God's terms just like me.
I must tell them if they want to go with dad, they must follow my lead.

At work, I display a new attitude that I am proud that everyone can see.
I will seek the future on God's terms and do something good for me.

At church, my spirit is high and my worship is directed from above.
I know that I receive agape love, and I return an agape level of love.

The criteria for perfection escape me.
But I know I can be as good as God expects me to be.

I will seek the future on God's terms and do something good for me.

Amazing Grace the Inner Peace

Amazing Grace shall always be our mom to praise.
For through our Grace--------- God sent her to give us inner peace.

We hope she knows-- just how much we love her so-.
Because she gave----- her time to fulfill our needs.

Chorus:

We shall greet----- her- when summer is in its highest--.
Or when the fields--- are covered white with snow-.

Yes, we'll be here ----in good times and in bad times.
To show our mom ----- just how much we love her so.

How wonderful ---this Grace that loved a helpless soul.
She followed God---- and brought us inner peace.

We shall forever------ send praises- up to Cal--vary.
To thank the cross for sending inner peace.

How wonderful this loves that saved our helpless soul.
For through God's Grace ---our peace has been made whole.

Chorus:

We shall greet----- her- when summer is in its highest--.
Or when the fields--- are covered white with snow-.

Yes, we'll be here ----in good times and in bad times.
To show our mom ----- just how much we love her so.

She Is Just a Baby

She is just a baby
A naïve young lady
That can't tell no from maybe.

She will be deceived because of selfish need
And a heart without love will bleed
Only God can save a lost seed.

She is just a baby
A naïve young lady
That can't tell no from maybe.

She was born with dangers around her.
Wolves wait to devour her.
Parents will neglect her.
And only God can love and protect her.

She is just a baby
A naïve young lady
That can't tell no from maybe.

Nobody will probably school the child
Because many want to use the child.
They only offer a deceptive smile
To this wanna-be woman child.

She is just a baby
A naïve young lady
That can't tell no from maybe.

The child will pick the wrong boy friend.
A wanna-be woman want to be with men.
Society show her sex is not sin.
She will live for today, not for the end.

She is just a baby
A naïve young lady
That can't tell no from maybe.

Whern her fear of pain is gone,
The game of lust is turned on.
When the deed is done, she will travel alone.
Unless it was God who made two one.

She is somebody's baby
A naïve young lady
That can't tell no from maybe.

A baby doesn't know anything about true love.
Must be taught it comes from above.
She doesn't know that lust will deceive her.
When it is too late, she will find that without God there is no love.

She is just a baby
A naïve young lady
That can't tell no from maybe.

What about Us

My Lord can sleep through a storm. What about us?

My Lord set the example of absolute trust but what about us?

What about you and what about me?
Can we hold it together in this stormy sea?

My Lord can sleep through a storm.   What about us?
The troubles of this world brought tears to my savior's eyes.
Now the troubles come double, but how many tears have you cried?

What about you and what about me?
Can we hold it together in this stormy sea?

My Lord can sleep through a storm. What about us?

My Lord can sleep through a storm; so can I.
My "Jesus wept" for the sad state of man –I know I can cry

My Lord brought good new to a dying world—so can I
He taught me I cannot fail if I try.

He told me my hand and my mouth must be linked to my heart.

What Did I Say

What did I say, -- what do I mean ------
Sometime talk --don't mean a thing----

What did you say-- what do you mean
be careful for it is not what it seems----

What did I do--- to deserve my God's goodness
I tell you all, I have been truly blessed----

If you praise God-- hold your head up high---
If it is from the heart it will reach the sky---

What did I say, --- what do I mean---
Sometime talk--- don't mean a thing----

If you love the Lord--- tell him how you feel.
When you walk for him, --- make sure it is real.

If you love the Lord--- praise him everyday
When your path is blocked, --- He'll make a way.

What did I say--- what do I mean ---
sometime talk--- don't mean a thing----

Heavenly Father

Hea-----ven-ly Fa-a--a---th-er hear--- my con---fes---sion

Hea-----ven-ly Fa------th-er hear--- my con---fes---sion

Fa--ther! I have so many sins
Father, please help me start over again

Fa--ther! Fa--ther! Have mercy please.
Thank you for bending my knees.

Hea-----ven-ly Fa----th-er forgive-- my trans-gres-sions.

My sins, my sins have traveled far and deep
Father, help me repent before I sleep

Hea-----ven-ly Fa------th-er hear--- my con---fes---sion

Father, Father make me listen to what You say.
Oh! Glorious Father teach me how to pray.

Hea-----ven-ly Fa----th-er forgive-- my trans-gres-sions.

Father! Make me understand my hope come from above.
Father! Oh! Father teach me how to love.

Hea-----ven-ly Fa----th-er forgive-- my trans-gres-sions.

Father! Show me how to reach others.
Help me, Father, to be a true brother.

Hea-----ven-ly Fa----th-er forgive-- my trans-gres-sions.
Hea-----ven-ly Fa----th-er forgive-- my trans-gres-sions.
Hea-----ven-ly Fa------th-er hear--- my con---fes---sion

XVI Acknowledgements

These poems were written for a special occasion. The occasion could be just to acknowledge or honor someone whether they are living or dead for a job done well, The occasion many times is a benefit for someone suffering from some dreaded disease. This list includes the following:

1. **The Unpretentious Man (A Methodist Minister)**
2. **Aunt Barbara, My Fairy-god Mother**
3. **The Eulogy (Rev. Roy, My Neighbor)**
4. **When One of Us Is Down (A Cancer Victim)**
5. **Because of the Spirit within Me (A Cancer Victim)**
6. **A Solicitous Man (A Church Member)**
7. **Sister Wash, the Faithful Saint (A Church Member)**

The Unpretentious Man

A man once humbled stepped into a lion's den and walked out.
He received praise but that is not what his trial was about.

His trial showed how humility could bring peace to a condemned man.
A humble spirit puts dread and apprehension in God's hand.

Then there were three humble spirits who were thrown into a furnace to burn.
Their humble spirits protected them from all harm…

A humble young man once picked up a stone and slung it true.
These exploits simply show you what humility will do.

In 1955 a humble lady took a seat at the wrong end of the bus.
The humble way she did it made her defiance just.

Once a humble young man denied powerful Potiphar's wife.
His profound humility probably saved his earthly life.
God inspired humility can remove all pain.
The road is expected to be rough for all who follow the man.

Humility is an outward sign of the followers of the man.
The best insurance falls under the humility plan.

Christ humbly carried his cross to the top of Calvary.
He gave the ultimate example of how to practice humility.

Look for the humility in the people around you.
The humble man is carrying the cross and you should follow suit.

This charge has been in the presence of a humble man for some time.
If he must go I know he will leave some of his humility behind.

I know this is what God wants him to do.
His job was to show us how to humbly carry the cross too.

He has told us and most of all he showed us how to humbly live.
He has given us much and he still has much to give.

We must take his example and share it with all.
He has done his job here and now must answer another call.

Rev. Dye, you have been a wonderful leader and someone we can call brother and friend
We are not going to worry about your soul, we know it is in good hands.

Rev. Dye, your humble spirit had identified you as a nice guy.
We do not know if we can measure up to you, but you have Motivated us to try.

We saw in you a God-centered plan for change.
Even a shared thought can erase great pain.

You have shared your thoughts with increased urgency and concern.
You have lit a small backfire in your attempt to stop a major burn.

Now it is up to us to fan the flame and burn away sin.
We may have enough time to shut the door to hell before it begins.

Thank you, kind sir, for being our Blessed leader.
We don't have much and we're not very many but call us if you need us.

Aunt Barbara, My Fairy God - Mother

A fairy tale is a special story when it is brought by a Fairy God-Mother.
I will never forget our story time on Drexel that we shared together.

You open my young mind to much of the world that I should have known.
Your stories were filled with life and gave me the essence that I still depend on.

Each supernatural story made my young mind seek relativity.
I found in them all a powerful life lesson I could adapt to me.

There was a definable good and bad theme that came right out at you.
I have no problem following righteousness because your stories told me what to do.

A fairy tale is a special story when it is brought by a Fairy God-Mother.
I will never forget our story time on Drexel that we shared together.

In the South we did not hug much, but in your world it was a standard greeting.
It was your world that taught me the value of a hug and it is still with me.

You would laugh and that would tell me we are having a great conversation.
Our good times together were like a concern Fairy God-Mother's intervention.

I will always remember the times we shared because it set my Love references.
I felt like a celebrity when you all waited at the train station for me.

I remember the Grit boxes and your little green and yellow Parakeet.
I'd taken baths before, but your bathtub was a first tub bath for me.

I learned the words "Soap Opera" from right there in your home.
You exposed a young mind to many fertile things to grow on.

You know I was quiet then because I had a bashful Love and a deep Soul.
You brought warmth and comfort to a child who was aware of a world that was cold.

A fairy tale is a special story when it is brought by a Fairy God-Mother.
I will never forget our story time on Drexel that we shared together.

I never say much because my Soul run deep into the here-and-now and eternity.
Jas 3:8 But the tongue can no man tame; it is an unruly evil, full of deadly poison.

I thank you Aunt Barbara, You have always been someone special to me.
God bless you, my Fairy God-Mother and Thanks for the Memories.

The Eulogy

He is gone now, no more pain.
But his life did produce a gain.

He chose not to put his formula for life in a letter.
Through his action, he showed you how to make life better.

Yes! My friend is gone to a better place.
This is a place of peace and only good days.

His physical body left us when he climbed to a heavenly home.
He leaves to cherish all his accomplishments which are not gone.

His accomplishments are shared by everyone.
We will all miss this man who was concern.

I shall always remember him saying "I am alright."

He was "alright" when he developed diabetes at 14 years old.
He was "alright" when they amputated his toes.

He was "alright" when gangrene developed in his feet.
He accepted the hand dealt him and never missed a beat.

He was "alright" when a foot had to be amputated.
He was alive and his spirit never abated.

Then it took everything except a stub below the knee.
With his new leg his spirit remained upbeat.

But he never stop saying "I am alright".
You would think he would be ready to call it a night.

"I am alright" appear to be all that he could say.
He never complained, not one moment in the day.

This man was beat down but each hardship he withstood.
He fought valiantly until this disease reached the source of life, the blood.

It silenced him for a time and he could not say "I am alright"
It was the "alright" that kept him alive; he peacefully lost the battle late one night.

When One of Us Is Down

From the time of our creation we never were suppose to walk alone. God has always watched over us and given us earthly hands to lean on.

Sometimes our trials come and it seems there is no end.
It is when we feel that all hope is gone; He will pick us up again.

And when one of us is down, God's solicitous saints will gather around.

They will say, "You are my sister and you are not alone.
Together we will get there and I will be your crutch to lean on."

When you fall, don't worry because God will catch you.
We walk with God; therefore we will be looking out for you too.

"Fear none of those things which thou shalt suffer" "for our God know thy works, thy labors, and thy patience" (Rev. 2:10; 2:2.)
Your trial is our trial, because our hope for the future depends on all our trials of the presents.

We are with you in spirit and with hearts full of Agape love.
We will surround you with a spirit that was sent from above.

It is the Holy Spirit that is within all of us that will be made stronger by the gathering.
When one of us is down, God's solicitous saints must gather around to pray and sing.

We will sing and pray because we love you and we want you to know. Our combined spirit-filled voices and prayers will cause all our blessings to flow.

We are committed to you like Ruth was committed to following Naomi.
Ruth's love for Naomi was so strong she had no fear of the unknown and wouldn't leave.

And when one of us is down, the commitment must come from all around.

And Ruth said and I quote:

Ruth 1:16 ………., Entreat me not to leave thee, or to return from following after thee: for whither thou goest, I will go; and where thou lodgest, I will lodge: thy people shall be my people, and thy God my God:

Ruth 1:17 Where thou diest, will I die, and there will I be buried: the LORD do so to me, and more also, if ought but death part thee and me.

"But death part thee and me", is strong Agape love from one person to another.
God expect this same love from each of us, toward our brothers and sisters.

We are your committed brothers and sisters who, for you, will do whatever it takes.
As we have opportunity, let us do good unto men, especially unto them who are of the household of faith" (Gal. 6:10.)

We must take your hand even if we have to carry you for a while. We stand with you in your anguish because we cannot help but to love God's child.

When one of us is down, you are not alone because we will gather around.

"And let us not be weary in well doing: for in due season we shall reap, if we faint not".
God has given us all His love and we will give you all that we've got" (Gal. 6:9.)

For "Thou shall love thy neighbor as thyself" is the second priority commandment.
We are all here because we love you and this day is a special day because it was heaven sent.

Your discomfort is our discomfort, but we will all be made the better for it.
Because we have learned how to live through discomfort from your gentile spirit.

And when one of us is down, we all must be prepared to gather around. This precious life we live will have some ups and there will be some down.

We hope our being here today has brought joy and happiness to your spirit.
Because we have come to say **we** love you, and we have brought joy to the Holy Spirit.

GOD BLESS YOU, MY SISTER and MAY OUR GOD BLESS YOU
With everything that you hope for.

Because it is the Spirit within me

Every discomfort my brothers and sisters feel;
it brings me pain that is beyond my will.

There is something working that we cannot see.
Because it is the Spirit within me.

Your pain is my pain be it big or small.
I feel what Jesus feels and He feels them all.

There is certainly something working that we cannot see.
I feel your pain because of the Spirit within me.

We are to wish you well, and to comfort you when you are down.
Our Spirit is to show you God's way to solid ground.

We are to tell you to have faith and only in God should you trust.
We can only show loving compassion, when the Spirit is within us.

We know there will be good time and bad time and pain will know everyone here.
It is the Spirit within us that allow each of us to care.

Today is your day and tomorrow another will be chosen.
But we must keep the faith because God has his reason.

It is that Spirit of God that guides us to surround you.
We hope the gathering of these Holy Spirits will help pull you through.

We all have access to the Comforter that will abide with us for eternity.
The purpose of God's church is to bring you comfortable peace.

We will take your hand and pray to our father in heaven that He blesses you.
We stand ready and willingly waiting to do whatever we must do.

We have faith in God and in His power we trust.
We share Jesus' compassion because of the Spirit in us.

I know there is a peace in this world but many cannot see.
I was led to this peace by the Spirit within me.

To Brother Ralph Hunter, my brother in Christ, from W. Thomas Love 1/13/2007

A Solicitous Man

We can meet people in passing and never really get to know them, but if we stay for a while and talk for a while, we can see and feel the soul of the person. To a Christian, life is burdensome and the more you care the heavier the burden. This man carried a heavy burden. He cared about us.
He knew where we as a people came from, but he was disappointed in the road we are traveling now. Caring for others is a heavy burden and if you don't believe it, my friend, then try carrying that burden for a while. This man cared because he knew how God intended us to live as neighbors. He wanted to utilize his God given talents to make a contribution to making this a better world, but there is little opportunity and less concern in a world gone mad in its quest to follow Satan's pleasures. His mind kept exploring and he kept wringing his hands in frustration. He wanted to say and may have said "what's the use" of continuing to try because nobody cares. He knew our situation with the youth today and he put the blame where it belongs; squarely at the feet of the adults. He looked beyond

traditions because it is traditions that have led us astray. He died looking for the truth, because he knew that it is the truth that would relieve his burden and the world's burdens.

To be solicitous is to be anxiously concerned. If you are solicitous, you will know frustration and you will wring your hands; and, yes, my brothers and sisters, you will cry. I never saw him cry but I felt his pain that was caused by a world without love. If you don't have love, you don't have his God. His God is the God that came down to earth as Jesus Christ. He loved his God. He told me about the time the church had so few members that only he and Brother King would meet to study the word; now that is commitment.

Sometimes it is the world that causes us to leave this earth and go to a heavenly home. Some of us cannot stand by and watch so many young and old people going to hell in a speedboat. Some of us will tell God, Father I have done all that I can but it continues to get worse. Some will even say, Father! They have even brought sin into your church. I try but I can't turn it around. When they tire of wringing their hand, and shed their last tear, they will say, Father I am ready to come home. And most of the time they silently slip away from a sinful chaotic world and go sit around the throne where they will know peace. Yes! Peace is a possibility! My friend!

To those who are here today under the traditional response called "Paying my Respects", let us pay a tribute to a soul that walked this earth and sought the truth of God. God sent this soul and we hypocritical souls frustrated this soul and it is time to change. We owe those who remain the **TRUTH OF GOD**. If you are not frustrated and wringing your hands, you need to pinch yourself because you are lost my friend and you do not care like Brother Lockett cared. Brother Lockett has finally found the peace he wished to enjoy while he walked the earth. Let us bring the peace of God to this earth, please Brothers and Sisters let us help the "Kingdom come".

Written 7/22/2009 in honor of Brother Randolph Lockett, our dear departed brother

Thanks my friend for the conversation and the concern,
W. Thomas Love

Sister Wash, the Faithful Saint

Sometimes when you are around a person, their **faith** gets in the way and you can't look any further than your perception of their belief. If you perceive holiness, you stop looking and simply label the person a **Saint**. You then let the person's holy character inspire you to become better. It is the continuous spiritual inspiration that drives you to look deeper because you want some of that holiness.

I don't remember the first time I met Sister Wash, but it was last year that I learned her name. I don't know if she walked with a cane the first time I met her because her **faith** was big and it overshadowed any physical limitations she might have had. Trying to understand her **faith** allowed me to see a perceived discomfort but I never heard her complain.

One thing that stood out which made her **faith** so strong was perseverance. Church meant a lot to her and it showed in her persistence. I remember her coming through the door using her walker with a determined look on her face. It was her steady persistent, ready for action attitude that masked her perceived disability.

Her **faith** and the way she displayed that **faith** showed us that her life's sole purpose was to bring glory to God. She brought glory to God in the life we saw; a life that lets us know that your life can speak for you. I don't know if she suffered because I could not see beyond her **faith**. I learned her last name early in 2008, but I had known her much longer. I only learned her first name in the latter part of 2008. There was no need for a name when she could have easily been called "**Sister Faith**".

We all need to honor her by bringing glory to God. It will take persistence and "a ready to work for God" attitude.

Written in honor of Sister Wash, a lady of faith, "Good bye, my sister"
W. Thomas Love, 9/3/09

XVII The Enterprise Area Pulpwood Haulers

There are stories or tales about the men who harvested the timber. The tales soon die shortly after the death of the woodman; this effort is to capture as much of the information as possible while it is still available. The harvesting of the timber included logging, pulp-wooding, crosstie and conduit. This document will tell parts of the lives of some notable wood harvesters and their extraordinary exploits. We hope to capture and present the lives of the woodmen. Today's machinery has replaced the brute strength that was required to work the woods. Men and animal was the primary means of harvesting the wood. This was hard work, and if one did not have the muscle when they started in the woods, they would soon develop the muscles. Many of the woodmen found in this presentation started their work in the woods very early; some were fifteen years old. We also interviewed the support network that made it possible to take wood to market. The main part of the network is the wood yard. The wood yards were primarily located at railroad tracks because wood was shipped by rail to the processing plants (Paper Mills). Lumber mills (saw mills) were localized processing plant that converted the wood into lumber. Many wood harvesters had their own saw mill. Cross-ties were squared in the woods with a broad-ax.

Figure 5 – The Pulpwood Truck with Loader

The Wood Yard

The following information came from **Mr. Andy Kersh**, the last owner of the Enterprise Wood Yard. This information is general information about the pulpwood side of wood harvesting:

- A cord of pine wood weighed in at 5200 pounds.
- A cord of hardwood weighed in at 5400 pounds.
- A stick of wood could weigh 500 pounds.
- A stick of pulpwood is 5 feet 3 inch long
- Wood was unloaded by hand from truck to train car in the early days.
- The Enterprise yard purchased the first mechanized unloader in the late 1950's or early sixties.
- Purchased the second unloader in 1967 and the last unloader in 1973.
- Measuring Stick was about ten feet.

- Mr. Frank Price ran the wood loader at the Enterprise Wood Yard. (Note: Ollie Lee Sanders said he pushed a 500 pound bail of cotton on Mr. Frank price and he carried it).
- Flinkote and Masonite of Laurel used to buy pulpwood ($15 to $20 dollars a cord).
- Mr. Henry Gray was a pulpwood man.
- Peter Earl was a hard worker and a good man. He would give you the shirt off his back.
- "Peter Earl and Ollie Lee Sanders would haul two loads of pulpwood and then load out 1000 square bales of hay".
- Mr. Bud Robinson used to haul pulpwood (Dwayne's dad).
- Robert Townsend was also a major pulpwood hauler.
- Sometime, between the hours of 12:00 noon to 1:00pm there were 30 trucks waiting to be unloaded. It took till 3:00 pm to unload them all and the person who was first was back with another load.
- Mr. Golden Hall would cut his wood with a buck saw and get someone with a truck to haul it for him. Mr. Robert Townsend hauled some of Mr. Golden wood.
- Mr. Albert Bradley hauled pulpwood.
- Mr. Roy Bradley hauled pulpwood

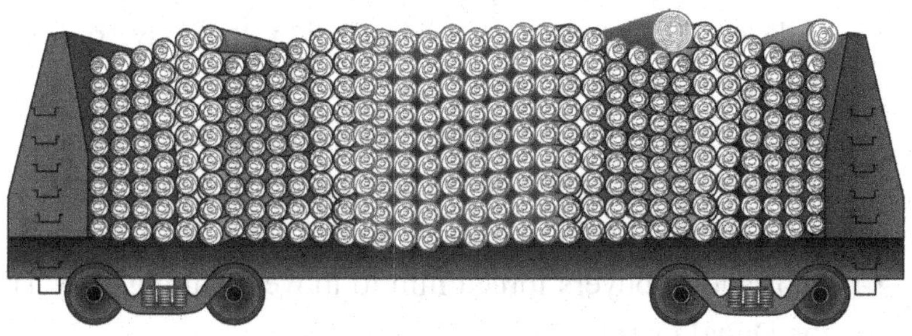

Figure 6 – The Wood Train

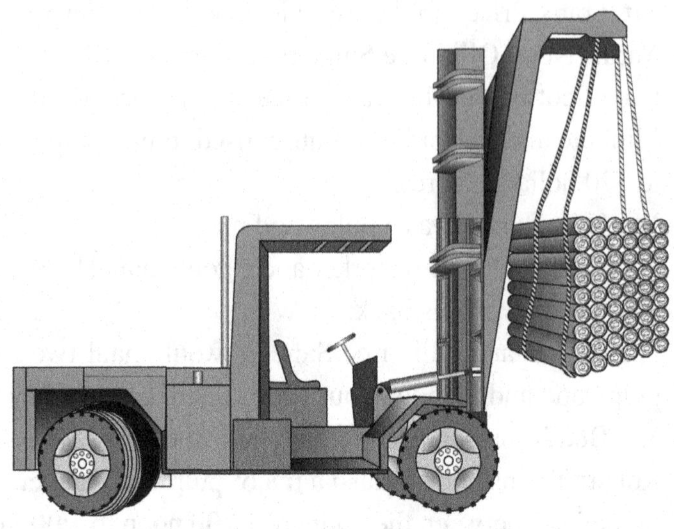

Figure 7 – The Loader/Unloader

The following information came from **Mr. Mike Culbreth** of the old Donald Wood Yard. This wood yard is located on Highway 513, North of Quitman.

- Length of pulpwood is 5 feet 2 inches
- Weight of a cord of pine is 5200 pounds
- Weight of a cord of hardwood is 5600 pounds.
- Hardwood is chipped up like pine to make paper.
- Only one at the time of this interview that buy traditional pulpwood length wood.
- Tree length is now replacing short wood; it pays more
- Tree length is shipped to the same place as short wood.
- Mr. Culbreth has been buying since 1991.
- Shortage of buyers forced him to move from highway 11 to the Donald yard.
- Use a 10 feet measuring stick.
- The height of the wood X (times) the length X (times) length of frame divided by 128 = a cord of wood will equal the units.

- Department of Agriculture set up the 128 constant.
- 9 feet wood is used for plywood – it is cut at the mill into 4 feet, 5 inches blocks.
- A stick of wood could weigh as much as 500 pounds.
- Mr. Robert Johnson consistently hauled 5.85 cords.
- Mr. Wayne Tools consistently hauled 5 and 6 cords.
- Petibone was the first unloader.

Mr. Marshall West, Donald Wood Yard clerk, added this information:

- Mr. West went to Pachuta Wood Yard in 1972 and purchased wood until 2001.
- Mr. West started hauling in 1959.
- Started buying in 1969.
- He knew the Edmonsons (W.C. and Johnny Lee), Mr. Roy Bradley because they haul to Pachuta.
- He leased his wood yard from the railroad.
- He had a contract with a paper company that directed where the wood is to be sent.
- The land owners are sent a stumpage copy or they come to pick it up.

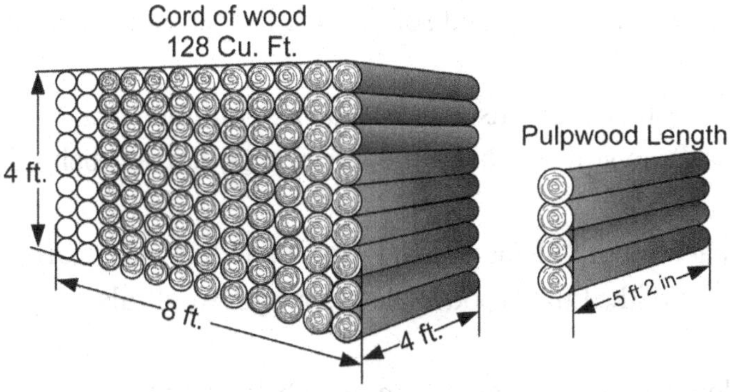

Figure 8 – Cord of Wood and Pulpwood Length

XVIII The Tale of the Enterprise Pulp Wood Haulers

Fiction will never tell the story about the men who fell the trees.
They were born to harvest the forest and then quietly leave.

The tale about Paul Bunyon was just a folksy story.
There are real men of the forest who received no glory.

These men of no glory were mighty men with independent minds.
They cut and hauled the hardwoods like the hickory and the soft pines.

The timber men were born to be haulers and they looked the part.
Some started out young and soft but the timber made them hard.

These were real Bunyons who will be lost in time.
The world can still see them in the fruit that they left behind.

The great strength of John Henry was a tale that was nearly true.
The stories of the Pulp Wood hauler's strength would also impress you.

John Henry was a confident man, who believed in himself.
The pulpwood haulers' basic needs were not left to someone else.

He did not have health insurance and he had to work to eat.
His best days always followed a good night of sleep.

The teenage boys were anxious to do the hard work.
They wanted the muscle that the pulpwood wood makes.

The youth works alongside the strong man to compare his growing arm.
The old pulpwood warrior has big muscles and the youth wants some.
The young men committed 110% to their work and their muscles quickly grew.
The major benefit from their legacy is what total commitment will do.

Remember the word commitment; it is required of any successful plan.
Commitment was the key to the strength of the pulpwood hauling man.

All pulpwood haulers were not the same, some commitment was hollow.
The great ones stayed the course and left a legacy to follow.

There is nothing wrong with work that is hard enough to bring sweat from the head.
Remember the curse that will bring sweat from your brow is a curse that God said.

The early pulpwood hauler's size was not an indicator of his load bearing ability.
Men of small stature had a tremendous wood carrying capacity.

Some men's frames were the size of growing children.
But these petite pulpwood haulers were mighty men.

Breakfast was a requirement to haul the pulpwood.
Some men's breakfast was not wholesome but they were good.

Men work together to push heavy wood on a single man.
He would carry it to the truck and threw if off his shoulders with his own hand.

The heavy load sometimes caused the derriere to tremble with every step.
This was too much weight for a human but these men sacrificed their health.
Carrying the heavy load strengthened the back, thigh, buttock, and triceps.
Bucking the heavy wood strengthens the latissimusdorsi, triceps and biceps.

The momentum of the wood was used to throw it onto the truck.
Rhythm and synchronization is utilized to remove the wood and pick it up.

Pulpwood hauling was dangerous work that brought death and injury both fast and slow.
The wood haulers were up to the task because they were "Mighty men of valor."

A tree would sometime fall and kill or injure a man.
The stacked wood would shift and crush a skull or hand.

The "Mighty Men of Valor" were on the front line of southern economic progress.
Regardless of the danger the men still worked with determination and boldness.

They got up early and stayed late to gather their allotted cords every day.
Overtime to the pulpwood hauler was cutting Monday's loads on Sunday.

To be successful in any labor requires self discipline and knowledge of the job.
Muscles gave way to technique and self-assurance gave way to faith in God.

Age is that common denominator that makes all men think.
Failure came to those who did not realize the brain does not function with the drink.

The bodies began to break and the mind lost time and speed.
The best of the class took care of themselves because they had mouths to feed.

The best worked the wood and did not let the wood work them.
Their insurance was awareness of the tree, stump and falling limbs.

Some had names they carried from their early childhood.
Some names seem to indicate that they were destined to cut the pulpwood.

There were names like Luther (Big Luke or Mic) Evans.
There was another big independent pulpwooder called Calton Pearson.

A tall slender strong man named Thayon (Jack) McMillian.
A muscle bound fellow from Toomsuba named Judson Jenkins.

Peter Earl, a shorter strong man who picked up a '57 Ford's rear.
Hal Mack loaded his truck tall like it had multiple tiers.

Mr. Rolinson, a white independent who hauled wood throughout his life.
Another life member who cut and hauled the trees is Mr. Book or Samuel Price.

Joe Bester, Jr., worked so hard on his two jobs it left his hairless head clean.
A whole family took to the woods with names like Spoke (Bill), Cotton
Blackie (Earl), Ribbin (Rueben Sr.), Allen and, Jeff Green.

Robert Lee Johnson or "Little Moley" came to Enterprise to haul wood with the men.
Lamar (Bud) Goins left the woodland of Enterprise and moved to Racine.

Mr. "R" Lee Sanders was still hauling wood until he was very old.
But a new attitude came to the woods in the young man, Wayne Toole.

Mr. Bill and Mrs. Pearl Green

Today is June 6, 2003, and there are only three of Mr. Bill Green's children left.
The majority lived into the eighties before they walked with death.

Mr. Bill and Mrs. Pearl McRae Green built a great black family.
They were taught very early that they could survive if they stayed close to the tree.

Mr. Bill was shorter than most of his sons, about five feet, eight inches.
He was strict with his children, and ill-will or junk from black or white he did not take.

The children respected Mr. Bill, therefore they did not want to fail.
They became productive citizens and tried to stay out of jail.

No one could come into Mr. Bill's house while obliviously drinking alcohol.
Mr. Bill did not tolerate any type of disrespectful attitude at all.

Mr. Bill Green was hauling back in the days when they used wagons. He would take wood to the Erwin Cotton Mill in Stonewall with his sons.

Mr. Rubin Green worked with Mr. Bill when he was twelve years old. The cotton mill used wood as a fuel just like the north used coal.

Five of the Green boys were drafted into the Army during World War II.
Most were called to serve their country and leave their family in 1942.

The recruits were Blackie, Allen, J.C., Rubin and Jeff.
They were all back home by 1945 and none lost to death.

Mr. Rubin started to work in the pulpwood industry in 1946.
This was shortly after he completed his 'hitch' in the military.

Mr. Rubin said he didn't "get much learning, and had to walk to school".
In the army, he became the trainer of truck drivers with God given brain tools.

Mr. Rubin became a corporal who worked a convoy in Burma, India. He stayed for eighteen months and he traveled far.

When Mr. Rubin was overseas, everybody acted just like brothers. But when he returned to Camp Shelby, he was called a nigger.

Mr. Bill Green was a contractor for an Enterprise sawmill.
He supplied the logs and moved the lumber to the Quitman kiln.

All of the Green boys worked with Mr. Bill before going out on their own.
They accepted what Mr. Bill paid them like loyal sons.

They ate a big hearty breakfast of milk, meat, eggs, coffee and occasionally rice.
The Greens did not eat grits, never were without food because Mr. Bill managed their life.

Mrs. Pearl sent a hot lunch to her family at the sawmill every day.
This Green family was a loving family who did everything the right way.

This family had plenty of cows and hogs and cured their own meat.
With a big smokehouse and a big farm, there was always plenty of food to eat.

This family would kill four or five hogs during killing season.
The Green family was so well organized that they did well during the Great Depression.

They would cook out two to three hundred pounds of lard.
A family cannot be this successful without a faith and trust in God.

From their own sugar cane, this family cooked out more than fifty gallons of syrup.
They had plenty of sweet potatoes and all the local vegetables that came from the earth.

Many of the boys were of the age to feel the effect of the depression.

At least three of the boys were older and Mr. Rubin was born November 1, 1921.

The Greens sharecropped during the Great Depression.
Mr. Rubin and Mrs. Emma could pick three hundred pounds of cotton.

Mr. Bill spent one thousand dollars in 1940 for a brand new Ford truck.
His success was based on hard work and management skills not blind luck.

Mr. Bill Green was the first Black man in the area to buy a model 'T' Ford.
Mr. Bill was a successful traveler over an impossible road.

Mr. Bill was the first Black man in the area to own a radio.
This man was a super achiever who showed his children how to grow.

Mr. Bill died after about seventy-two years of very successful days.
Mr. Bill Green did not just talk success to his sons, he showed them the way.

Mr. Rubin Green

Mr. Rubin Green started hauling pulpwood on his own in nineteen forty-six.
He bought a $4,000 truck on time as a young man of twenty-six.

He bought the truck through Donald's Wood Yard.
He was to pay for the truck at the rate of two dollars per cord.

This truck was very unusual because it had a loader mounted on it.
The buck-saw was the device used to cut the pulpwood sticks.

In 1947, the buck-saw was put out to pasture by a David Bradley from Sears & Roebuck.
Mr. Rubin could pull four cords of wood on his new truck.

He would receive $9.00 per cord after the $2.00 deduction.
Each load brought Mr. Rubin a total of thirty-six dollars honorarium.

Gasoline cost 20 to 30 cents a gallon and the helper $5.00 for a 12 hour day.
At $108 for three loads in the 1940's is more than outstanding pay.

Mr. Rubin went to work in the cotton mill in Stonewall.
He had to go back to the woods because his income took too much of a fall.

Mr. Rubin soon hauled three to four loads at four cords each a day.
The average of two loads is a good estimate of his pay.

Mr. James Donald told him when he had overpaid for his truck.
He was hauling wood so fast that the $2.00 per cord quickly mounted up.

A brother could work for a brother for six dollars a day.
In the forties, that was good money and more than regular pay.

Mr. Bill Green's children learned to work hard for their living.
Mr. Rueben said that he never knew any of the Greens being turned down for anything.

He also said, "We Greens would do what we said we would do".
The Green name was a trustworthy name too.

We did not talk about who came before Mr. Bill and Mrs. Pearl.
These two people were giants who produced some truly outstanding boys and girls.

This family was a role model that many blacks failed to see.
By working together, the whole family excelled far beyond basic needs.

Mr. Rubin is the last of the brothers and he was eighty-one at the time of the interview.

Mr. Earl (Blackie) Green

Mr. Blackie Green, Mr. Jeff and Mr. Cotton were loggers (logs are measured in the 1000 feet because they are longer).

In the 1940's loggers were paid $40 per 1000 feet.
The landowner was paid $10 per 1000 feet for the stumpage of the tree.

Logs were delivered to local sawmills not to the train.
Logging was a bigger operation that required the skitter, mules and man.

A typical trailer truck could haul about 3000 feet of logs each trip.
Ninety dollars a load was good money destined for the pocket on the hip.

Mr. Blackie and Mr. Jeff worked together with two mules and two trucks.
They also had a logging train or skitter with 300 feet of line to pull the logs up.

Mr. Cotton worked by himself with one truck and a pair of horses.
He never used a power saw but his smaller operation minimized his loses.

At Sanders Lumber Company, a load of logs fell on Mr. Jeff.
Doctors said he would never walk again because of a broken pelvis.

Mr. Spoke hauled pulpwood with two trucks, but not by himself.
He kept his operation going with determination and lots of hired help.

The Green Family made some remarkable achievements.
They were a family who worked together in a God approved way and success was heaven sent.

The Green boys honored their father and their mother in every way.
All but two lived into their eighties, and living to the promised day.

J.C. or Peter Rabbit and Allen Green died from heart failure.
Nobody knows why God gives long life to some and select others.

Allen worked the woods; also his claim to fame was the conduit.
Conduits are the horizontal cross arms on the telegraph pole, not pulpwood.

In the 40s or 50s Mrs. Blackie cut cross-ties at his own sawmill
He was making a lot of money on the Masonite timber hills

The government caused him to shut it down because of the money track
He did not pay his men social security and he had problem with income tax

Mr. Harold (Hal) Mack

Another life-time member of the pulpwood Hall of Fame was Hal Mack.
He started to work the woods early, and never looked back.

Mr. Harold played all the angles because he was a man of self-reliance.
Hal was a thrifty man who prepared for life's future slumps and tests.

He did his own mechanical work and owned a welder, too.
Hal was aware of the world because he served in World War II.

Mr. Harold did not like anybody telling him what to do.
As his own boss, he set the course and pulled each job through.

Hal raised cattle and hogs for food and supplemental income.
Farming fed the family, fed the animals and he sold some.

Hal buffered his life for everything to go his way.
His thriftiness was saving for that rainy day.

One day while cutting wood, Hal was bitten by a rattlesnake on the ankle.
One of his workers took him to the Quitman hospital.

This day he encountered two snakes, he cut one and the other bit him.
Snakes are always a threat to the pulpwood haulers' limbs.

Hal was a self-made man who accumulated his property and farm animals.
He married Ms. Rosie Lee Pearson and fathered two males and a female.

Hal preferred the Ford cars and the Ford trucks.
Hal used the skitter truck to pick the heavy wood up.

Mrs. Rosie Lee had breakfast ready at 6:00 a.m. and Hal was on time.
It did not matter if the weather was cold or hot, Hal kept to the time line.

Hal would say "If you make one dollar, put twenty-five cents back". Hal did not have the stability of a large family but something put him on the right track.

His farm was organized and he had everything under control.
He had cribs, smokehouses and a house to keep his birthing sows out of the cold.

He did not work with the other haulers, he got his own contracts.
Most pulpwood haulers were independent and looked after their own back.

Harold had a colon cancer but only he knew for how long.
He told the doctors that he was going to fight it out; he did not want to be cut on.

God gave him time to get right with Him and Hal helped to build a church.
Hal was a dying deacon who tried to give God's hand more than a touch.

They found Harold early one Saturday morning lying on the floor.
He was gasping and trying to talk but then his eyes rolled back and he let go.

September 25, 1911 to November 14, 1987

Mr. Calton Pearson

Mr. Calton Pearson was another pulpwood hauler who worked the woods all his life.
There may be a connection because Mrs. Emma Green is his wife.

He is the oldest of six children, with three sisters and two brothers.
His children are the beautiful Mary Rose and one other daughter.

He worked only one truck with hired help.
He would operate his skitter himself.

Mr. Calton also used mules in the woods in the early days.
He looked to the future because his social security was paid.

Mr. Calton is eighty-five years and doesn't get around so well.
He was sixty-five when he ran out of wood to sell.

Mr. Paul Rolison

Mr. Paul was another man who spent his life cutting the trees.
He worked other jobs but gave them all up for the woods in the early fifties.

He was a loner who wanted to be his own boss.
He was not a big man, his first truck did not have a loader but he understood the cost.

The cost includes physical exertion, pain and lots of time.
He took to the woods like a man with a made up mind.

Mr. Paul always had a power-saw, which made his solitary effort a possibility.
His World War II army training assured him of his capability.

Mr. Paul and Mrs. Lola Ruth had a precious little girl at the time he began cutting the trees.
He managed his life as a church going loner with three mouths to feed.

He usually worked alone but sometimes he hired big Luther Evans, a pulpwood man.
Mr. Rolison thought the world of this gentle giant with the trust worthy hand.

He always arose at about 6 a.m. and ate a hearty breakfast.
Pulpwood is heavy and food is necessary to make the effort last.

Sometime he would hire Mr. John Smith to help him cut the wood.
Mr. Paul did not work with everyone, only men he understood.

He grew up in Enterprise and was a member of Union Baptist Church.
He would pull people out of ditches at all times of the night because he cared that much.

Mr. Paul's greatest joy was Janice, his "baby" girl.
He called her "baby" most of the time because she completed his world.

On October 15, 1972 at 4:00 a.m., Mr. Rolison's world changed.
This was the time that death sneaked upon Janice and took her name.

The pine forest grew blacker than a cypress swamp the night Janice died.
This tragedy devastated the family to the point it seems the dog cried.

Champ, the German shepherd, started howling four hours before she left.
Somehow this family pet had a premonition of the beloved Janice's death.

The beautiful Janice died from a heart attack at only twenty-four years old.
She was born at 4:00 a.m. and died at 4:00 a.m., six years after marriage to Mr. Bobby Joe Moulds.

Mr. Paul never really recovered from the loss of his only offspring.
He went back to the woods with a broken heart and the trees had changed.

Mr. Paul may have had early health problems but they never left his mind.
He seemed to think the problems would go away in time.

He was an avid church goer which could probably explain a self-healing belief.
Twelve years after Janice departed this life he made preparation to leave.

Mr. Paul developed an aneurysm that brought him unbearable pain.
The trip to the V.A. hospital meant he would never enter the woods again.

The end came April 10, 1994, at 4:00 o'clock on a Sunday.
Mr. Paul and Mrs. Lola Ruth spent 52 years together—a long stay.

Mr. Golden Hall

Mr. Golden lived a life centered on resources of his own creation.
Pulpwood helped to provide the capital to run his small farm.

Mr. Golden would cut three loads of pulpwood in a week.
He worked alone with a buck saw and ax to accomplish this feat.

His load consisted of 3 units of wood that were 5 feet, 2 inches long.
In 2003 Mr. Golden was 86 years old and still living in his daddy's home.

He hauled wood to Mr. Bennie Kersh and Mr. Johnson for 22 years. He never got hurt and sometime he would work with Mr. Willie Ferrell.

In 1938 he helped to build Highway 11 at wages of 221/2 cent per hour.
His duty was to pave the road with a shovel and man-power.

His self-sufficient life style included raising hogs and cattle for meat and income.
He was his own helping hand because he had only one daughter and no son.

This is the life of a man who worked pulpwood, the farm and the road.
His life epitomized self-sufficiency and how a man carries his own load.

Mr. Samuel Price

Mr. Sam is the oldest of the pulpwood men and is in the best physical shape.
I believe his long successful life came from his ability to calculate.

A man doesn't live eighty-five plus years unless he evaluates life's risk.
In an occupation of many dangers, even minor potentials can't be missed.

Mr. Sam has proven that a man must stay on his toes to stay on his feet.
He shows himself friendly because he does not know who he is going to meet.

The time is April 21, 2003, and Mr. Sam still drives to Enterprise and Stonewall.
He sits high in his red pickup because he is over six feet four inches tall.

Mr. Sam will wave, blow his horn and project his strong voice.
Mr. Sam never met a stranger as if he had no choice.

Mr. Sammy started hauling pulpwood when he was seventeen.
For more than fifty years, he worked in a world of green.

Mr. Tucker Berry was that old strong man that introduced the young Sammy to the trees.
Mr. Berry must have taught him well because it took Mr. Sammy fifty years to leave.

From 1936 to 1986 is a long time to carry the heavy wood on even the strongest back;
With double work of on-loading in the woods and off-loading at the railroad track.

Mr. Sammy worked with his head because he never hurt his back.
He never tried to manhandle the wood, his lifting technique was always right.

Mr. Sammy never got his back in an awkward position or strain.
Handling pulpwood without a loader could cripple or kill a man.

Mr. Sammy worked by himself mostly but his brother-in-law helped him five years.
Being his own boss gave him time to work the cotton field.

He raised 8 to 10 bales of cotton at sixty dollars a bale.
He raised his own meat, lard, syrup, vegetables and some to sell.

The worst woodcutting was done around lakes.
The wood was no problem; the problem was the moccasin snakes.

The "old rusty moccasins were bad, knew they came at you".
One sneaked up on his brother-in-law but he told him what to do.

The rattlesnake pilot was found on the hillside, ready to strike.
In the wood, the hauler had to look up, down, to the front and to the back.

Mr. Sammy came from a line of woodsmen.
He was in the woods when his grandpa used four oxen.

The lead oxen were used to pull the fallen tree to the temporary road.
A "cross hog" and chain was on the truck to load.

Mr. Sammy remembers a brand new Chevrolet truck with four wheels.
Four wheels turned to six wheels to carry the loads over the hills.

Mr. Sammy took his loads to Enterprise and unloaded by hand.
Mr. Fairchild was the wood yard and telegraph pole man.

Mr. Sammy saw a truck run over Mr. Peter McClain and kill him.
He was dragged into the path of the moving truck by a limb.

Mr. Sammy carried his lifeless body to the road and called Bennie Straihome.
Pulpwood hauling is dangerous work that takes lives and breaks bones.

In 1948, Mr. Sammy bought his first truck that he would crank by hand.
Even the trucks were dangerous, because they would break the hands of man.

Some fifty-six years ago Mr. Sammy made Mrs. Willie Elmer Smith his wife.
A faith in God has given them ten children and a wonderful and blessed life.

Mr. Willie J. Dillard

Mr. Willie J. Dillard started hauling the pulpwood when he was very young.
In nineteen ninety-three at seventy-one years of age, his pulpwood hauling
Days were done.

When he was born, the midwife said he was not going to live.
Somehow he has survived to the age of eighty-one and worked hard for Sixty-six years.

Late in life, the doctor said he had pneumonia when he was born.
Mr. Dillard has a clear mind and a sound body for a man of eighty-one.

He never broke a bone as he worked among the tall pines.
Working with his dad, Mr. Jessie gave him peace of mind.

He and Mr. Jessie worked with just one truck.
One could cut with a bucksaw while the other picked it up.

Mr. Willie liked Chevrolet trucks because he thought they were more dependable.
The cross-cut saw was also used to cut the daily yield.

If the cross-cut saw was not level, the up man was riding.
Riding was tough on the low man, and brought on complaining.

The Dillards got their first power saw in the sixties.
The power saw could cut wood too big to carry.

Some large sticks were pushed on a man and kicked off of him.
These were the trunk of trees not the limbs.

They took their wood to Enterprise, Meridian and Quitman.
It was tough to unload the trucks because it was done by hand.

They would pull along beside the rail car and flip the wood on it.
This was a slow process because the flipping was done stick by stick.

They tried to make it to the wood yard before it closed for the evening.
It was a better day when the truck started empty in the morning.

It was a disheartening sight to see all the rail cars "loaded-out or full".
They were directed to other wood yards that might be buying wood.

Some haulers were directed to other yards for less than honorable reasons.
Exploitation was a way of life and always in season.

The wood haulers joined hands and went to a Jackson court to voice their grievances.
The way wood was bought and their money was being compromised by thievery.

One outcome was that the wood yard could not refuse to take the wood.
When it came to standing up for justice, Mr. Willie Dillard stood.

The wood haulers were asked to stand together and Mr. Willie Dillard stood.
Mr. Willie sold wood by weight and he sold it by measurement.

Whether by weight or measurement, Mr. Willie sold his wood.
This was a family venture.

Mr. Jessie Dillard was a logger before he started out on his own.
Mr. Jessie's pulp wooding grew to its independence with the growth of his sons.

The Dillard family proved that a family that hauled together stayed together.

Mr. Ollie Lee Sanders

Mr. Ollie Lee (RLee) Sanders is another man who spent his life with the tree.
He started cutting the tree when he was sixteen and now he is seventy three.

Mr. 'R' Lee started with the Green brothers, a family of timber men.
The Green brothers worked the woods like the farmer works the land.

In 1945, Mr.'R' Lee went to the woods with new muscle and much to learn.
He started to work the pulp-wood with Mr. Gene Burk in 1951.

Mr. Burk's operation hauled with two and some three trucks.
Mr.'R' Lee would cut the trees down while others pick them up.

This job was a job that paid by the day.
In 1961, Mr. 'R' Lee worked ten hours in the woods for $5.50 a day.

Mr.'R' Lee started work at 7:00AM and sometimes worked until 6:00 o'clock.
There was no overtime pay but when the rain came his pay was docked.

Mr. 'R" Lee was the guy who really cut the tree. He was the saw-man.
He kept his file, oil and an ax, and a gasoline can.

Mr.'R'Lee stopped working for Mr. Burk after nineteen years.
Mr. Burk paid into his social security because it was the government's will.

He left Mr. Burk in 1968 and struck out on his own.
He owned over eight trucks up until 2000 and he primarily worked the woods alone.

He worked with Mr. Kersh in his later years at 75 or 80 dollars a day.
The better wages were good but the social security was taken away.

Pulpwood hauling was hard and dangerous that broke many bones.
In his early year, Mr.'R' Lee hurt his leg and broke his arm.

He got hurt while working with Mr. Andy Kersh and was paid $300.00 every two weeks.
He was taken to Anderson Hospital when he was hit by a small tree.

Mr. 'R' Lee was hauling pulpwood when he was seventy years old.
The old man worked by himself and daily he would still get two loads.

When you work by yourself, you are the saw-man, loading-man, and hauling-man, too.
Fifty-five years of cutting, hauling and loading will show the pulpwood man what he must do.

Mr. Babe Pete

Baby Pete is another legendary pulpwood hauling man.
He was very young when he started to work the timber land.

At fourteen years old Baby Pete bought his own truck.
He hit the wood with zeal and never gave up.

His brother, Bubby gave him the name Baby Pete.
He was a slender fellow, who stood one inch over six feet.

Baby Pete lived in the fast lane and hung out with men who were older.
He had six brothers and the baby boy Don was two inches taller.

The fourteen year old Baby Pete grew to be recognized for his strength.
He was good with the baseball bat and bad with the lug wrench.

Baby Pete and strong man Peter Earl were competing friends.
Baby Pete and Peter Earl were pulpwood made men.

Gambling and fast or loose women were his major vices.
One day at the Cool Breeze he and Peter Earl tied up while shooting dice.

Peter hit Baby Pete with a gallon jug of moonshine.
These two were fighting friends at the time.

Baby Pete loved to drive his cars and trucks very fast.
Where others hit the brakes, Baby Pete hit the gas.

Baby Pete turned over several trucks loaded with wood.
The danger associated with speed he never understood.

Baby Pete turner over several cars in his quest to get there quickly.
He would outrun the state trooper and Mr. Prince if only he could stay out of the ditch.

Baby Pete was a feared man because he would not back-down from a fight.
It was said if you mess with Baby Pete, you best not turn your back.

Two of his favorite weapons were the jack handle and bat.
He had the determination of the pit bull and the stealth quickness of the cat.

The man didn't smoke and didn't get his courage from alcohol.
He could stay out late and when morning came he was ready to haul.

Baby Pete hit Shelly Cole with a bat and caused him much harm.
One night at the Cool Breeze, Shelly paid him back with a shot in the arm.

He rode to the hospital in his trunk to keep blood off his seat.
The cleanness of his Cadillac car was more important to Baby Pete.

Baby Pete's real name was Thayon (Jack) McMillan.
In September 1, 1969, Baby Pete died with a bullet in him.

Additional information contributed by others:

- Babe Pete was a hard worker.
- Young men looked up to him and he taught them how to drive.

- He was a nice dresser.
- He loved to dance.
- He was brought up independent.
- He had at least 4 outside children.
- He talked about women.
- He played cards.
- He gambled.
- He did not misuse anybody.
- He did not let anybody misuse him.
- He died as he lived
- An Incident: "Babe Pete asks for lady J. but the young lady would not tell him. So, he took a fire poker and hit her across the arm".

The Olivers (Butt Cut)

This information came from **Mr. Earnest Oliver**. The interest in a woodman named Mr. Anthony Oliver leads to this writing. Mr. Earnest was killed in a head-on automobile accident in November, 2006. See Figure 9 for an illustration of a "ButtCut."

Mr. Anthony Oliver was an impressive logging man.
He had large draft horses that stood about 20 hands.

He would drive through the town of Enterprise with his truck stacked very high.
Mr. Oliver loads were so impressive that it caught even the child's eye.

Mr. Anthony was short and stocky, much like the pine tree butt.
His broad powerful shoulders earned him the name "Butt Cut"

Mr. "Butt cut" always had a place to unload and orders to fill.

His daddy-in-law, Mr. Munch would buy wood from Mr. "Butt cut" for his sawmill.

Mr. Huston Oliver was Mr. "Butt cut's" uncle and he also depended on animals for pay.
Mr. Huston's mules sloped the bank of the New Highway 11 and loaded 3 boxcars of logs a day.

Mr. Huston had a total of five mules, 2 for the woods and 3 for the farm.
There was lot of work to go around because he raised 17 bales of cotton.

Farming and logging is two jobs he could not do by himself.
He had 9 boys and 3 girls for the farm and hired 3 men for logging help.

Mr. Houston would leave his mules in Mr. Pink Brown's barn because they were for hire.
In 1930, his mules worked the highway and later they were used to stretch telegraph wire.

With such animal friends Mr. Houston was never alone.
In fact he could turn his mules loose in town and they would go home.

This was an Eden type of relationship that the whole community could see.
He was so close to his animals he gave them names like George and Henry.

These mules were smart and knew when the wagon was full.
When the load got heavy one of the mules would grab brush in his mouthy to pull.

This type of relationship between man and beast is not possible without God's touch.
Mr. Houston was close to God because he was a steward in Magnolia Church.

The Oliver brothers included one who rode the rails from Meridian to New Orleans.
He was a big shot with money that had an appropriate name of "King".

The time was 1930's and the train would stop everywhere.
When Mr. King's train stopped in Enterprise his mother would always be there.

Mr. "Butt cut" moved away to Florida in his later years, and was killed by a cable. Mr. King Oliver was called a "Big Shot" because he made approximately ten dollars a month. This was a lot of money for a black man in the 30s (1931 – 1939). He would board the children from Enterprise in his home when they came to New Orleans

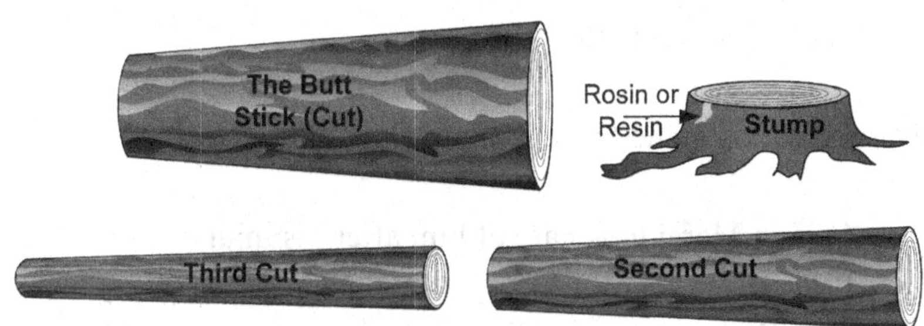

Figure 9 – The Butt Cut

Mr. Peter Earl

There was a legendary pulpwood hauler who died in 1995 at 60 years of age. He is known for his generous attitude and his great strength. Peter Earl is his name. Peter is buried in the same community where he was born, Bethel community. Peter's mother was named West Duck and she had five children; Peter, Mary, Martha, Annie and Bertha.

This information came from Mr. Hill (Manson).

- Mrs. West Duck raised Peter on Church Street.
- Mr. Lee Doby was Peter's first cousin.
- Peter's aunt was named Lizzie (Lee Doby's mama)
- They were part Indian
- There were Hardys on the grandma's side.
- Peter's daddy was Dick Earl.
- Mrs. West Duck and Mrs. Lizzie were Hardys.
- Mr. Sam Earl was Peter's first cousin.
- Peter never drank alcohol.
- A tree hit him in the nose area.

This Information came from William Dyess (Tubby):

- Cousin Marai took care of him after his injury.
- Peter never got over his injury to his face area (nose).
- Dick Earl was double-jointed which may account for his great strength.
- Peter was born on the Kemper Plantation in the Bethel community.
- Peter went to the Bethel school.
- William Dyess said, "Peter picked up a '64 Chevy that he own and removed it from a ditch."

This statement came from Robert Evans:
Mr. Buddy Richburg bet Peter Earl that he could not lift a ten feet section of railroad track rail. He lifted it and carried it across Highway 11. This was witnessed by the following individuals:

1. Albert J. Price
2. Johnny Robert Overstreet
3. Johnny Lee Edmonson

Robert also said, Spruce Pine is heavy wood; but Iron wood is the heaviest, and it grows in rebreaks.

Other Comments about Peter from various sources.

- Peter Earl picked up a full-dress 289 engine from Johnson Enterprises. They would not help him load it, so he put it on his shoulder.
- Peter and Ollie Lee purchased timber together.
- Peter would carry the butt-stick even when he had a loader. (Ollie Lee Sanders)
- Peter lifted up the back of a car so a person could change a tire.
- "He could lift anything; loaded wood at the wood yard".
- Peter Earl gambled – he hit Babe Pete with a gallon of whisky during a dispute over a dice game.
- "Peter Earl and Ollie Lee Sander would challenge each other as to who could pick up the biggest stick of pulpwood. Sometime they would take it of the railcar and put it back" (Daryle Edmonson)
- Peter picked up a car that was in the ditch (Mr. Earnest Price)
- While jacking up a car, jack slip and Peter grab drive shaft to stop it from rolling. (Mr. Earnest Price)
- Peter would carry the butt-cut. (Mr. Earnest Price)

- Peter picked up the front part of a mule while Manson was sitting on the mule.
- He was a nice person who would help you. (John Curtice Hill Jr.)
- "Peter had a thing for Desiree Thomas Goines"
- "Peter never had much book learning but common sense. Could take engine, backend and transmission apart.
- "Don't know how the tree hit him but he had a bruise place on his shoulder blade".

Figure 10 illustrates the wood midway through the "Bucking" technique. This right-handed person used his left leg and left arm to swing (kick) the left-end of the wood over his head to his shoulder. Once the wood is kicked upward, it never stops until it lands on the shoulder. The right hand is the controlling hand. Peter Earl would use this technique to lift wood because he often worked alone.

Figure 10 – Peter Earl would carry (Buck) the Butt-Cut

Peter's pulpwood work came to a tragic end while working the woods. One day he was cutting a tree and a limb fell and hit him in the lower part of his face. He was able to walk out of the woods but he had to go to the hospital. Figure 11 is illustrating how this probably happen.

Figure 11 – Falling Limb and Falling Tree

Peter was never able to return to the wood. According to William "Tubby" Dyess, cousin Mariah took care of him and he never got over the injury to his face area. Figure 12 is was described of Peter's injury.

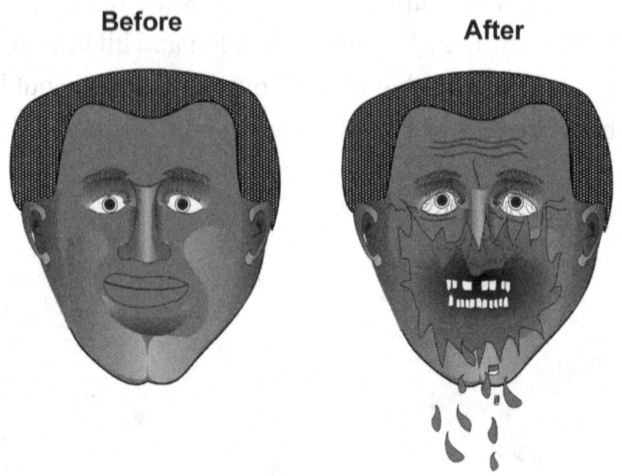

Figure 12 – Peter's Injury

"Death in the Woods" is a true account of the death of Henry Louis King. Henry Louis was a very intelligent young man who was accidently killed while hauling pulpwood. His story was told by the only surviving eyewitness.

Death in the Woods (As told by Larry Evans)

The place, a pine forest in Lauderdale County, and the time was August 22, 1969;
This was a good day for harvesting the trees and a poor day for dying.

The forest shall strike back this day from the darkness of a deep ravine. The pulpwood truck was topped-out by three men and a boy who was nearly nineteen.

The woods were deep, more than a mile from Mama Lou and the Hi-way 59's Savoy exit.

The full truck slowly climbed out of the steep ravine but then all forward progress quit.

Peter Earl and Baby Pete, as senior woodmen came up with a plan. The plan was to let the struggling truck's winch system give it a helping hand.

This winch system was very unique because the boom was located above the cab of the truck.
The boom operator could sit on the cab to operate the winch as it picked the wood up.

Larry Evans was the third adult who worked the woods that faithful morning.
The song, "Sometime I Feel like a Motherless Child" is what Larry was singing.

Baby Pete asked Larry to operate the winch to help pull the truck up the hill.
Larry said he couldn't because he did not have boom operating skills.

Henry Lewis King was eighteen years old and due to have a birthday soon.
While Baby Pete drove the truck, Henry Lewis was chosen to operate the boom.

They hooked the boom's cable somewhat diagonal to the truck's path.
Henry Lewis pulled with the winch as Baby Pete stepped on the gas.

The motor raced and tires spun as the truck struggled to pull itself through.
The cable from the winch became as rigid as a steel bar as the winch pulled too.

The motor and the boom system struggled to pull the loaded truck up the hill.
Like the flash of lighting, time stopped and the woods became dark, quiet and still.

Two sounds were heard, that of a loud snap and that of a gentle thud.
It took the body forever to fall among the pieces of brains and blood.

The cable had snapped causing the boom to open the left side of Henry Lewis' head.
The brains trailing from his head was a clear indicator Henry Lewis was dead.

Baby Pete got out of the truck and rushed to Henry Lewis' side.
Baby Pete looked as deeply troubled as the scene that lay before his eyes.

Baby Pete told Larry to take some newspaper and cover him up.
Baby Pete ran to get help while an extremely distressed Larry stayed with the truck.

After what seemed like an eternity, Larry heard voices coming through the trees.
Soon he heard the rapid footsteps of people on the fallen leaves.

Through the undergrowth the first human Larry saw was Henry Lewis' mother.
Not far behind her was the coroner, sheriff and other men with a stretcher.

Bootsie, Henry Lewis's mother, looked as if she expected some sign of life as a tear fell from her eye.
Reality soon set-in as Bootsie slowly kneel down to whisper her final goodbye.

Tushing King, Henry Lewis' father came to the place of his fallen love one.
A distraught Tushing told Baby Pete, "You killed my son!"

The body was released to Enterprise Funeral Home after the investigation.
Baby Pete, Larry Evans and Peter Earl accompanied the family and body on this solemn occasion.

Figure 13 – Henry Lewis using Boom Cable to Pull

Figure 14 – Cable Broke and Henry Lewis Fell

This information was added by Dr. Claude McGowan

Class of 1969 had 10 year reunion and the class presented her with a gift.

- Henry Lewis' girl friend was Lorene Newman.
- Lots of young people at the funeral.
- His mother seems to age early with his death.
- Henry Lewis was probably the smartest person in the class but spent much of his time cutting up in class.
- He was going to go to Harris Jr. College.
- He always sweated on his nose.
- He was always well dressed.
- He often went to Racine, Wisconsin, for the summer.
- May have been with Baby Pete when the Earl boy got killed.
- He came back from Racine and died within two weeks.

Dr. Annie L. Burns added this information.

Henry Lewis was a brilliant student based on grades, how he carried himself and articulation. He drank a little. He was worried how his mom perceived his potential for failure. He had returned from Racine after working in a factory there for the summer. His plan was to go to school. He was distracted by something but not sure of what it was but he was aware of his problem. He would talk to Annie Lou.

The Big Tree Fell

From a whack and a slash the big tree fell.
Kill by the strong men who wanted wood to sell.

death came slowly but its final act was profound.
There is no racket like the racket of a big tree lying down.

Sometimes the falling tree kicks and takes men down with them.
The mighty tree sometimes turns, break and throw a limb.

From a whack and a slash the big tree fell
Killed by the strong men who wanted wood to sell.

Four hundred years of growth must relinquish life
In minutes the saw will cut through the tree like a knife.

It seems the tree has a sort of vengeful will.
Its limbs have been known to cause men to be crushed by the truck wheels.

From a whack and a slash the big tree fell.
Killed by the strong men who wanted wood to sell.

When the big tree falls, there has got to be pain.
The pain of the tree falling and the pain of picking it up again.

I wonder how the other trees feel as they see the neighbor fall.
Is there the attempt to shrink or does the tree continue to stand tall.

From a whack and a slash the big tree fell.
Killed by the strong men who wanted wood to sell.

What if the trees are the trees of life.
Then every wasted tree will shorten someone's life.

God planted these trees and they must be honored as a sacred thing.
Listen to the foreboding warning the doomed tree sings.

From a whack and a slash the big tree fell.
Killed by the strong men who wanted wood to sell.

Two man lift and carry technique:
Much of the wood was too heavy for one man too pick up. The men would work in pairs to lift the wood but one man would carry the heavy wood. The process of lifting the wood was called "Pushing it on". As the figure (Figure 15) below illustrates, the man who is to carry the wood bends down to lift and his shoulder acts as a fulcrum. As he lifts the standing person pushes in an upward manner and provides a counter-weight effect on the lift. Once the wood is on the person shoulder he can carry it.

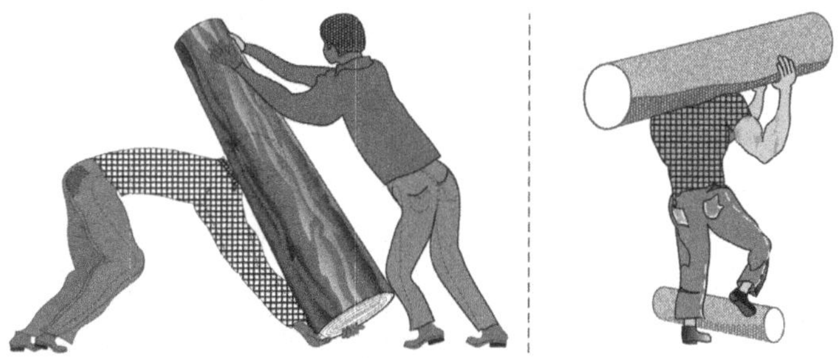

Figure 15 – Two Man Lift and Carry

Long wood has taken the place of short wood. In the past we called the long wood logs. Figure 16 is an illustration of the equipment used to load the long wood.

Figure 16 – Long-wood Loader

Printed in the United States
By Bookmasters